London Travel Tips For First-time Visitors

Maariya .E Mccaffrey

Introduction

London, a city with a rich tapestry of history, culture, and modernity, beckons travelers with its unique blend of old-world charm and contemporary vibrance. As a destination that has something for everyone, London's allure lies in its ability to constantly evolve while preserving its heritage with utmost pride. This guide aims to equip travelers with essential insights, ensuring a memorable journey through the heart of the United Kingdom.

The history of London is as fascinating as it is long. From its origins as a Roman settlement to its status as a world capital of culture, finance, and politics, the city's past is palpable in its architecture, museums, and cobblestone streets. Exploring London is akin to walking through a live history lesson, with landmarks such as the Tower of London, Westminster Abbey, and the Houses of Parliament offering a glimpse into the city's storied past.

Navigating London is made easy by its extensive public transportation network. The London Underground, affectionately known as the Tube, is an efficient way to travel across the city. Buses, trains, and the iconic black cabs provide alternative means of transportation, each offering a unique way to experience London. For a more scenic route, the River Thames offers boat services, allowing travelers to see the city from a different perspective.

Among London's most famous attractions are the Buckingham Palace, the London Eye, and the Shard. These landmarks not only define the city's skyline but also offer visitors a chance to experience the royal heritage, panoramic views, and architectural innovation that London is known for.

Museums and galleries abound, catering to all interests. The British Museum, the Tate Modern, and the National Gallery showcase collections ranging from ancient artifacts to contemporary art, reflecting the city's global cultural influence. Admission to many of London's museums is free, making it possible for visitors to immerse themselves in art and history without a hefty price tag.

London's parks, such as Hyde Park, Regents Park, and Hampstead Heath, are referred to as the 'green lungs' of the city. These vast expanses offer a peaceful escape from the urban hustle and bustle, with lush landscapes, serene lakes, and winding paths perfect for leisurely walks or picnics.

For those who delight in retail therapy, London's shopping districts like Oxford Street, Regent Street, and Covent Garden offer an eclectic mix of high street brands, luxury boutiques, and quaint market stalls. Notting Hill, with its famous Portobello Road Market, offers antiques and vintage finds, showcasing the city's diverse shopping experiences.

Accommodations in London cater to a wide range of preferences and budgets. From luxurious hotels to cozy bed and breakfasts, and even budget-friendly hostels, finding a place to stay is easy, with each neighborhood offering its unique charm and convenience.

London's culinary scene is as diverse as its population. Foodies can indulge in traditional British fare, such as fish and chips and afternoon tea, or explore the myriad of international cuisines available throughout the city. Borough Market and Brick Lane are just two examples of destinations where food enthusiasts can enjoy a variety of flavors from around the world.

The nightlife and clubbing scene in London is vibrant and diverse, with venues catering to every musical taste and ambiance. From historic pubs to cutting-edge nightclubs, the city comes alive after dark, offering endless entertainment options.

London, with its mix of historical sites, cultural institutions, green spaces, shopping districts, diverse cuisine, and lively nightlife, promises an unforgettable experience for every traveler. Whether you're visiting for the first time or returning to discover more, London's charm is bound to captivate your heart.

Contents

Chapter 1: All Roads Lead To London

London is the most served destination in the world when it comes to flights. With a total of six international airports, of which only two are located within Greater London, there are a number of other regional UK airports conveniently accessible from London. Considering they offer a growing number of budget flights, choosing those airports can be cheaper or even faster, depending on your exact destination in London.

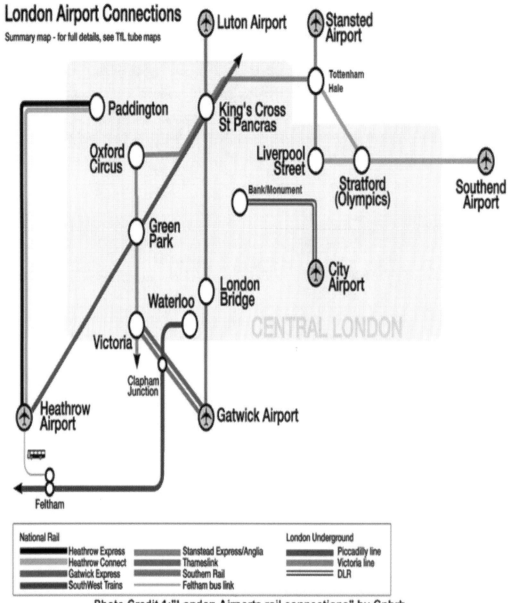

London Airport Connections

Summary map - for full details, see TfL tube maps

Luton Airport

Stansted Airport

Tottenham Hale

Paddington

King's Cross St Pancras

Oxford Circus

Liverpool Street

Stratford (Olympics)

Southend Airport

Bank/Monument

Green Park

City Airport

London Bridge

Waterloo

CENTRAL LONDON

Victoria

Clapham Junction

Heathrow Airport

Gatwick Airport

Feltham

National Rail		London Underground	
Heathrow Express	Stanstead Express/Anglia	Piccadilly line	
Heathrow Connect	Thameslink	Victoria line	
Gatwick Express	Southern Rail	DLR	
SouthWest Trains	Feltham bus link		

The airports are conveniently interconnected by a large number of public transport links. For transfers directly between London's airports, the fastest way (short of a taxi) is the direct inter-airport bus service by National Express. However, make sure to allow leeway, as London's expressways are often congested to the point of gridlock.

London Heathrow Airport is the busiest airport in the United Kingdom and the busiest airport in Europe by passenger traffic. Heathrow is also the third busiest airport in the world by total passenger traffic. Heathrow, London's primary airport, is located 23 kilometers west of central London, near the south end of the London Borough of Hillingdon. Only Heathrow and London City Airport are within Greater London.

It's a giant, sprawling airport currently divided into five terminals (T1, T2, T3, T4 and T5). It is so large; in fact, it could almost qualify as being a small city in itself. This is why there is a significant internal transport system. All travel within the airport boundary on local bus and Heathrow Express & Connect

Photo Credit 2:"Heathrow Express train" by Andrew Butcher
Licensed under CC BY-SA 3.0 via Wikimedia Commons

trains is free.

No matter what your preferences are, Heathrow offers plenty of public traffic connections to Central London. Heathrow Express trains leave every 15 minutes for the 15-minute journey to London's Paddington station. It's the fastest way but also by far the most expensive. Actually, it is one of the most expensive train journeys in the world. Oyster Cards and London Travel cards are not valid for Heathrow Express. Trains depart from Heathrow Terminal 5 station or Heathrow Central station (Terminals 1, 2 and 3). A Heathrow Express transfer service operates between Terminal 4 and Heathrow Central to connect with services from London and Terminal 5. The first train from Heathrow leaves at 05:42AM and the last at 11:42PM.

The trains are air-conditioned, modern, and comfortable, and they are fully accessible with a wheelchair area, disabled toilet and level access to the station platforms. Free Wi-Fi Internet access is also available on board. On board TV entertainment plays throughout the journey, but for those who'd like some peace, quiet zones are also available

Tickets can be purchased in advance online, from the station or on-board the train. They vary in price depending on where you bought them. An Express Class Adult Single bought online costs £16.50 or £18.00 at the station with a £3 surcharge over the at-station price if you buy on-board. A return ticket costs £32 online or at station. Child fares (5-15 years inclusive) are about half the adult fare. Children under 5 years of age travel free.

Heathrow Connect trains leave every 30 minutes for the 27-minute journey to Paddington. The trains leave directly from Terminals 1, 3 & 4, and via a connection from T5. This service uses the same route to London Paddington as the Heathrow Express but this is a slower, less frequent train which also serves intermediate local stations in West London. The Heathrow Connect provides a convenient connection to London Underground's Central Line at Ealing Broadway station. The first train from Heathrow leaves at 5:23 AM and the last at 00:01AM.

London Travel cards and Oyster Cards are not valid between Hayes & Harlington and Heathrow Airport. Passengers holding a Travel card or Oyster Card must buy an additional ticket for the journey between Hayes & Harlington and Heathrow. The ticket price between Hayes & Harlington and Heathrow is £4.90 Adult Single. All tickets must be purchased before boarding the train and will be checked on board. Those without one will have to pay a penalty fare. The tickets can be bought at station ticket offices. A Heathrow to London Paddington Adult Single costs £8.50 while an Open Return is £16.50. Child fares (5-15 years inclusive) are about half the adult fare. Children under 5 travel free.

The trains departing from Terminal 4 stop at Terminals 1 & 3, Hayes & Harlington, Southall, Hanwell, West Ealing and Ealing Broadway. The trains are air-conditioned, modern and accessible with a wheelchair area and disabled toilet. Audio and visual journey information is available on-board. Mobile phone coverage is available throughout the route, including in the tunnels under Heathrow.

South West Trains run every 20 minutes. Oyster cards are valid on these trains. There is a bus link from Terminals 1, 2 & 3 (bus 285) and Terminals 4 & 5 (bus 490) to Feltham railway station. Although a slower route, if you are heading for South London or West London suburbs, Richmond or Windsor, this could prove a useful shortcut. Depending on the route, some trains take 30 minutes others take 45 minutes, so it is advised to check the train times carefully if you are rushing. You must buy your train ticket before boarding as this is not an airport express train but a standard suburban rail service.

London Underground's Piccadilly Line Direct to Central London runs up to every 5 minutes, depending on the terminal. The Piccadilly Line runs direct from all the terminals to the very centre of London, stopping at stations close to many of London's landmarks, shopping and entertainment areas, as well as the major transport hub at King's Cross St. Pancras. Trains depart from Terminals 4 and 5 every 10 minutes and stop at Terminals 1 and 3 before continuing to London. It stops frequently and is comparatively slow. It takes about an hour from Terminal 5 to King's Cross St. Pancras. However, it is an integral part of Transport for London's network so Travel cards and Oyster Cards are valid, making it a good value option. It's also a fairly quick option if you want to reach parts of West London. The Tube closes during the night and the first trains leave Heathrow at about 6AM, while the last trains are around midnight. As The Tube is a rapid transport system designed with short journeys in mind, the trains are not the most comfortable. However, from Heathrow there will almost always be seats available and luggage space is provided. There is space for wheelchairs and the Heathrow stations are accessible, but as The Tube is an old system originally built in the 19th century, very few stations in Central London are accessible to wheelchairs. Audio and visual journey

information is provided on board.

Photo Credit 4:"Piccadilly line carriage" by GK tramrunner229 Licensed under CC BY-SA 3.0 via Wikimedia Commons

The Tube is a closed system and nearly all stations have ticket barriers. Tickets should be bought at the station and the cost of a Zone 1 - 6 (Central London - Heathrow) single ticket is £5.50. Travel cards are available and will almost certainly provide better value if you plan on using London's transport system more than a couple of times. The cheapest option for anyone spending much time in London will probably be to get an Oyster Card.

Coaches are available every 30 minutes to London Victoria Coach Station. National Express runs a direct coach service from Heathrow Central Bus Station to London Victoria Coach Station. The journey time is 40 to 50 minutes and fares are available from £4 if bought online. Tickets can also be bought from the National Express ticket office at Heathrow Bus Station. Some services operate via Terminals 4 and 5, but this service is more limited. Free transfer is available to Terminals 1 and 3 and the Central Bus Station. London Travel cards and Oyster Cards are not valid. They operate from 7AM to 11:30 PM.

Fares vary depending on the operator, but Transport for London services (red buses) are subject to the standard £2.00 flat fare when paying by cash. Travel cards and Oyster Cards are also valid on these buses.

During the night, one of the few ways you can get to and from Heathrow is by using the N9 night bus service. The service runs every 20 minutes on weeknights and takes around 1 hour and 10 minutes to Heathrow Central Bus Station and continues to Terminal 5. The service is operated using modern, accessible, low-floor busses with a wheelchair space. The fare is £2.00 and Travel cards and Oyster Cards are valid on these buses.

London's famous black taxis are available outside each terminal. Journey time to Central London varies depending on distance, time of day and traffic conditions. It can take anything from 40

minutes to 2 hours. Fares vary similarly, but as a rough guide it should cost about £55 to Central London. Minicabs (private hire cars) must be ordered in advance by phone or online. Usually they cost less than a black cab. If you are thinking of taking a taxi to London, consider the Heathrow Express and you can pick up a taxi at Paddington Station to complete your journey. Dot2Dot is also an option. They will probably be faster and cheaper, and almost as easy to use.

Gatwick Airport is London's second-largest international airport and the second-busiest by total passenger traffic in the United Kingdom. It's located 47.5 kilometers south of Central London in West Sussex. It's split into a North and South Terminal. The two terminals are linked by a free shuttle train that runs every 5 minutes.

There are plenty of transportations options from Gatwick Airport. The train station is located in the South Terminal. Gatwick Express runs every 15 minutes with a journey time of about half an hour. The tickets to Gatwick Express are the most expensive. A better option may be Southern Railway. The trains leave every 15 minutes. The journey time is 35-40 min. All services between Gatwick and Victoria are operated by Southern Railway. The time saving on the "Express" trains compared to the normal services is minimal. There is also little differentiation in on-board comfort. Southern Railway also operates services to Milton Keynes in the north of London. These trains use an orbital rail line through the Earls Court area and avoid central London.

Thameslink is cheaper than any other rail option. But there is a major rebuilding program affecting London Bridge station. The work should be completed by 2018. Thameslink provides direct trains to Luton Airport. For many destinations in central or east London, the Thameslink services are a better option, usually quicker and cheaper.

The most reliable bus option is National Express. It leaves every 30 minutes and has a journey time of around 75-110 minutes.

If you decide to take a Minicab it'll cost you around £70 and an hour and a half to two hours of journey. For most visitors, choosing the trains makes the journey to Central London significantly quicker.

London Stansted Airport is the third busiest airport in London, located at Stansted Mountfitchet in the district of Uttlesford in Essex, 48 kilometers northeast of Central London.

If you happen to land on Stansted Airport there are plenty of options available that will get you to where you need to go. Stansted Express trains leave to London Liverpool Street every 15 minutes, with a journey time of 45-60 minutes. A one way ticket costs £23.40, a round trip £33.20. You can get better deals if you book 7 days in advance or travel in a group. Oyster and Travel cards are not valid. You could also take Stansted Express to Tottenham Hale and then switch to Victoria line in the Tube. This route is also quicker if you're heading to South London, the West End or West London. You can get an Oyster card at Tottenham Hale which is a more economical way of moving rough London.

National Express buses leave every 15-30minutes. The journey time to Stratford is 1 hour, to Victoria 90 minutes. To Stratford (tube: Stratford) or Victoria (tube: Victoria). The ticket to Stratford is £8 one way and £14 round trip. To Victoria it's £10 one way and £16 for a round-trip. Travel card or Oyster cards are not valid. Terravision also provides buses. A ticket to Liverpool Street or Victoria is £9 in one way, £14 round trip. A one way ticket to Stratford is £6 while a round trip ticket is £11. Travel cards and Oyster are not valid.

You also have the option of taking a minibus. EasyBus can take you to Baker Street. But these buses are not recommendable as the company turned out to be very unreliable. Buses are usually overbooked. The tickets go from £2 if you purchase them online in advance to £8 for a one way ticket. Travel card or Oyster are not valid.

Since this airport is pretty far from Central London, it's usually better and cheaper to go by train. A taxi will take about an hour and a half and approximately cost you £70.

London Luton Airport is physically much smaller than Stansted, but still a major hub for many Low Cost airlines as over 10 million passengers fly through the airport each year. The airport lies a few miles away from the M1 motorway, which runs southwards to London, northwards to Leeds and connects to the M25 motorway.

The airport has its own railway station "Luton Airport Parkway". It's served by trains 24 hours a day from Central London using "First Capital Connect Trains" and connects with St Pancras International. There are up to 10 trains an hour, depending on the time of day. All trains go to London St Pancras International, but many also continue on to Blackfriars, London Bridge and Elephant & Castle, Gatwick Airport and Brighton. The station is nearly 2 kilometers away from the terminal building, but there is a shuttle bus service running between the terminal and airport every 10 minutes. Journey time is 20-55min and the ticket costs £13.50 one way. Travel cards are not valid.

You can also get a bus, Green Line number 757. The bus leaves every 20 minutes and the journey should take around 90 minutes. It stops at Victoria (tube: Victoria) via Brent Cross, Finchley Rd tube station, Baker St, Marble Arch and Hyde Park Corner. The ticket is £14 one way if you get it from the driver. Travel cards are not valid. You can also use National Express, It eaves every 2 minutes with a journey time of about 90 minutes. It stops at Victoria (tube: Victoria) via Golders Green and Marble Arch. One way tickets go from £1 if you buy them online in advance. Travel card is not valid.

London City Airport It is located in the Royal Docks in the London Borough of Newham, some 11 kilometers east of the City of London and a rather smaller distance east of Canary Wharf.

You may find that from some origins, this may be your cheapest London airport to fly to, without even considering the cost savings of NOT coming from the distant larger London airports with £10+ transfer costs.

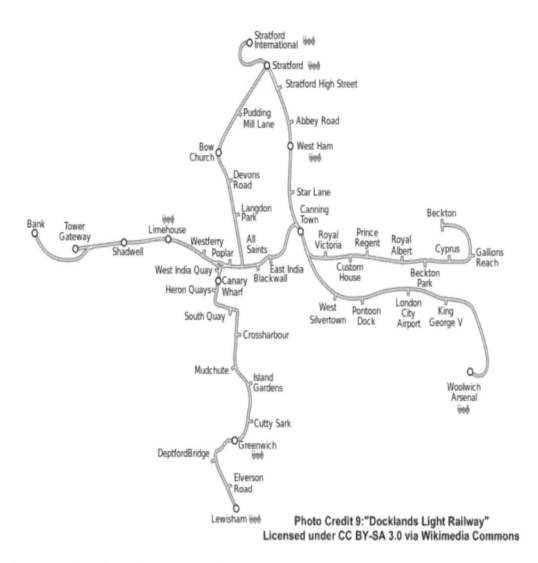

Photo Credit 9:"Docklands Light Railway"
Licensed under CC BY-SA 3.0 via Wikimedia Commons

It's linked to London's new financial district at Canary Wharf, to the traditional financial district of the City of London, and to Stratford International station adjacent to the Olympic Park, via the Docklands Light Railway, that offers interchanges with London Underground, London Overground, TfL Rail, Abellio Greater Anglia, c2c and Southeastern High Speed train services. London City Airport DLR station adjoins the terminal building, with enclosed access to and from the elevated platforms. Travel cards are valid.

The airport is served by London Buses services 473 to Stratford via Plaistow and North Woolwich and 474 to Canning Town and Manor Park via Beckton and East Ham. From Canning Town take the 115 or N15 into central London. Travel cards are valid.
If you decide to go by taxi it will take you roughly half an hour and cost around £20-35.

London Southend Airport is located in the district of Rochford within Essex, approximately 68 kilometers from the centre of London. It serves a range of destinations in Europe and the British Isles.

The airport has its own railway station "Southend Airport", and is served from Liverpool Street, via Stratford by trains 17 hours a day. There are up to 8 trains an hour, depending on the time of day. The station is located some 200 meters from the terminal building. The journey time takes about 55-65 minutes. Travel cards are not valid.

Chapter 2: History Of London

It is considered unlikely that a pre-Roman city existed, but as some of the Roman city remains unexcavated, it is still possible that some major settlement may yet be discovered. London was most likely a rural area with scattered settlement. Rich finds such as the Battersea Shield, found in the Thames near Chelsea, suggest the area was important.

Some discoveries indicate probable very early settlements near the Thames in the London area. In 2010 the foundations of a large timber structure, dated to 4000BC, were found on the Thames foreshore, south of Vauxhall Bridge. In 199

Photo Credit 11 "Battersea Shield" by Babel Stone Licensed under CC0 via Wikimedia Commons

9, the remains of a Bronze Age bridge were found, again on the foreshore south of Vauxhall Bridge. This bridge either crossed the Thames, or went to a now lost island in the river. Dendrology dated the timbers to 1500BC. In 2001 a further dig found that the timbers were driven vertically into the ground on the south bank of the Thames west of Vauxhall Bridge. Numerous finds have been made of spear heads and weaponry from the Bronze and Iron ages near the banks of the Thames in the London area, many of which had clearly been used in battle. This suggests that the Thames was an important tribal boundary.

Londinium was established as a civilian town by the Romans about seven years after the invasion of AD 43. London, like Rome, was founded on the point of the river where it was narrow enough to bridge and the strategic location of the city provided easy access to much of Europe. Early Roman London occupied a relatively small area, roughly equivalent to the size of Hyde Park. In around AD 60, it was destroyed by the Iceni led by their queen Boudica. The city was quickly rebuilt as a planned Roman town.

At some time between 180 and 225 AD the Romans built the defensive London Wall around the landward side of the city. The wall was about 3 kilometers long, 6 meters high and 2.5 meters thick. The wall would survive for another 1,600 years and define the City of London's perimeters for centuries to come. The perimeters of the present City are roughly defined by the line of the ancient wall. Isolated Roman period remains and traces of the wall are still to be seen within the City of London (now known as the Square Mile). In the late 3rd century, Londinium was raided on several occasions by Saxon pirates. This led, from around 255 onwards, to the construction of an additional riverside wall.

By the 5th century the Roman Empire was in rapid decline, and in 410 AD the Roman occupation of Britain came to an end. Following this, the Roman city also went into rapid decline and by the end of the 5th century was practically abandoned.

After the end of Roman rule in 410, London experienced a gradual revival under the Anglo-Saxons. A coalition of Angles, Saxons and Jutes from Northern Europe, the Anglo-Saxons ruled in Britain for 500 years until the Norman invasion of 1066. The early Anglo-Saxon trading settlement of Lundenwic was established a mile away from Londinium. London's British Museum houses the largest collection of Anglo-Saxon artifacts in the world.

Viking attacks dominated most of the 9th century, becoming increasingly common from around 830 onwards. London was sacked in 842 and again in 851. The Danish "Great Heathen Army", which had rampaged across England since 865, wintered in London in 871. The city remained in Danish hands until 886, when it was captured by the forces of King Alfred the Great of Wessex and reincorporated into Mercia, then governed under Alfred's sovereignty by his son-in-law Ealdorman Aethelred.

Around this time the focus of settlement moved within the old Roman walls for the sake of defense, and the city became known as

Lundenburgh. The Roman walls were repaired and the defensive ditch re-cut, while the bridge was probably rebuilt at this time. A second fortified Borough was established on the south bank at Southwark, the Suthringa Geworc (defensive work of the men of Surrey). The old settlement of Lundenwic became known as the ealdwic or "old settlement", a name which survives today as Aldwych. From this point, the City of London began to develop its own unique local government. Following Aethelred's death in 911 it was transferred to Wessex, preceding the absorption of the rest of Mercia in 918.

Although it faced competition for political preeminence in the United Kingdom of England from the traditional West Saxon centre of Winchester, London's size and commercial wealth brought it a steadily increasing importance as a focus of governmental activity. King Aethelstan held many meetings of the witan in London and issued laws from there, while King Aethelred the Unready issued the Laws of London there in 978. Following the resumption of Viking attacks in the reign of Aethelred, London was unsuccessfully attacked in 994 by an army under King Sweyn Forkbeard of Denmark. As English resistance to the sustained and escalating Danish onslaught finally collapsed in 1013, London repulsed an attack by the Danes and was the last place to hold out while the rest of the country submitted to Sweyn, but by the end of the year it too capitulated and Aethelred fled abroad. Sweyn died just five weeks after having been proclaimed king and Aethelred was restored to the throne, but Sweyn's son Cnut returned to the attack in 1015.

After Aethelred's death at London in 1016 his son Edmund Ironside was proclaimed king there by the witangemot and left to gather forces in Wessex. London was then subjected to a systematic siege by Cnut but was relieved by King Edmund's army; when Edmund again left to recruit reinforcements in Wessex the Danes resumed the siege but were again unsuccessful. However, following his defeat at the Battle of Assandun Edmund ceded to Cnut all of

England north of the Thames, including London, and his death a few weeks later left Cnut in control of the whole country.

Following the extinction of Cnut's dynasty in 1042 English rule was restored under Edward the Confessor. He was responsible for the foundation of Westminster Abbey and spent much of his time at Westminster, which from this time steadily supplanted the City itself as the centre of government. Edward's death at Westminster in 1066 without a clear heir led to a succession dispute and the Norman conquest of England. Earl Harold Godwinson was elected king by the witangemot and crowned in Westminster Abbey but was defeated and killed by William the Bastard, Duke of Normandy at the Battle of Hastings. The surviving members of the witan met in London and elected King Edward's young nephew Edgar the Aetheling as king.

The Normans advanced to the south bank of the Thames opposite London, where they defeated an English attack and burned Southwark but were unable to storm the bridge. They moved upstream and crossed the river at Wallingford before advancing on London from the north-west. The resolve of the English leadership to resist collapsed and the chief citizens of London went out together with the leading members of the Church and aristocracy to submit to William at Berkhamstead, although according to some accounts there was a subsequent violent clash when the Normans reached the city. Having occupied London, William was crowned king in Westminster Abbey.

The new Norman regime established new fortresses within the city to dominate the native population. By far the most important of these was the Tower of London at the eastern end of the city, where the initial wooden fortification was rapidly replaced by the construction of the first stone castle in England. The smaller forts of Baynard's Castle and Montfichet's Castle were also established along the waterfront. King William also granted a charter in 1067 confirming the city's existing rights, privileges and laws. Its growing self-government was consolidated by the election rights granted by King John in 1199 and 1215.

In 1097 William Rufus, the son of William the Conqueror began the construction of 'Westminster Hall', which became the focus of the Palace of Westminster.

In 1176 construction began of the most famous incarnation of London Bridge (completed in 1209) which was built on the site of several earlier wooden bridges. This bridge would last for 600 years, and remained the only bridge across the River Thames until 1739.

Over the following centuries, London would shake off the heavy French cultural and linguistic influence which had been there since the times of the Norman Conquest. The city would figure heavily in the development of Early Modern English.

Trade increased steadily during the Middle Ages, and London grew rapidly as a result. Medieval London was made up of narrow and twisting streets, and most

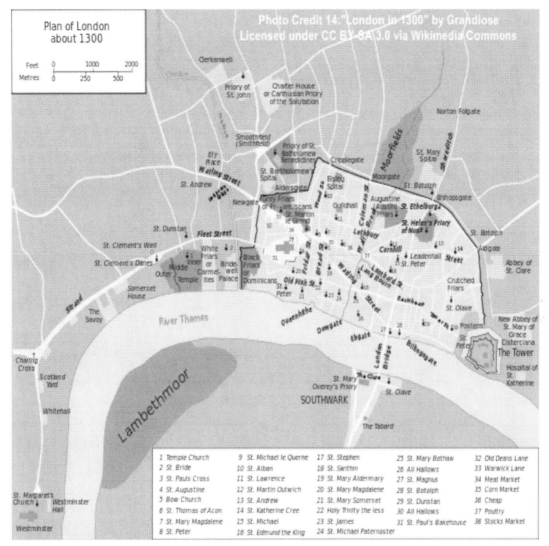

Plan of London about 1300

Feet	0	1000	2000
Metres	0	250	500

1 Temple Church	9 St. Michael le Querne	17 St. Stephen	25 St. Mary Bothaw	32 Old Deans Lane
2 St. Bride	10 St. Alban	18 St. Swithin	26 All Hallows	33 Warwick Lane
3 St. Pauls Cross	11 St. Lawrence	19 St. Mary Aldermary	27 St. Magnus	34 Meat Market
4 St. Augustine	12 St. Martin Outwich	20 St. Mary Magdalene	28 St. Botolph	35 Corn Market
5 Bow Church	13 St. Andrew	21 St. Mary Somerset	29 St. Dunstan	36 Cheap
6 St. Thomas of Acon	14 St. Katherine Cree	22 Holy Trinity the less	30 All Hallows	37 Poultry
7 St. Mary Magdalene	15 St. Michael	23 St. James	31 St. Paul's Bakehouse	38 Stocks Market
8 St. Peter	16 St. Edmund the King	24 St. Michael Paternoster		

of the buildings were made from combustible materials such as wood and straw, which made fire a constant threat, while sanitation in cities was poor.

During the Reformation, London was the principal early centre of Protestantism in England. Its close commercial connections with the Protestant heartlands in northern continental Europe, large foreign mercantile communities, disproportionately large number of literate

29

inhabitants and role as the centre of the English print trade all contributed to the spread of the new ideas of religious reform.

The period saw London rapidly rising in importance amongst Europe's commercial centers. Trade expanded beyond Western Europe to Russia, the Levant, and the Americas. This was the period of mercantilism and monopoly trading companies. The growth of the population and wealth of London was fuelled by a vast expansion in the use of coastal shipping.

London's long association with the theatre flourished during the English Renaissance (late 15th to early 17th C). From 1576 indoor and outdoor theatres began to appear in London. The Rose Theatre was built in 1587 in the reign of Elizabeth 1st and was the first purpose-built theatre to stage the plays of Shakespeare. The most famous outdoor theatre was the Globe, built in 1599 by The Lord

Chamberlain's Men. William Shakespeare was their resident playwright. Admission prices ranged from a penny standing charge to sixpence for the most desirable seats. There are currently over forty London theatres in the West End, in an area known as 'Theatreland'. London's Victoria and Albert Museum houses a permanent exhibition of the history of British theatre.

London's expansion beyond the boundaries of the City was decisively established in the 17th century. In the opening years of that century the immediate environs of the City, with the principal exception of the aristocratic residences in the direction of Westminster, were still considered not conducive to health. The general meeting-place of Londoners in the day-time was the nave of Old St. Paul's Cathedral. Merchants conducted business in the aisles, and used the font as a counter upon which to make their payments; lawyers received clients at their particular pillars; and the unemployed looked for work. St Paul's Churchyard was the centre of the book trade and Fleet Street was a centre of public entertainment. Under James I the theatre, which established itself so firmly in the latter years of Elizabeth, grew further in popularity. The performances

at the public theatres were complemented by elaborate masques at the royal court and at the Inns of Court.

Charles I acceded to the throne in 1625. During his reign, aristocrats began to inhabit the West End in large numbers. In addition to those who had specific business at court, increasing numbers of country landowners and their families lived in London for part of the year simply for the social life. This was the beginning of the "London season". Lincoln's Inn Fields was built about 1629. The piazza of Covent Garden, designed by England's first classically trained architect Inigo Jones followed in about 1632. The neighboring streets were built shortly afterwards, and the names of Henrietta, Charles, James, King and York Streets were given after members of the royal family.

In January 1642 five members of parliament whom the King wished to arrest were granted refuge in the City. In August of the same year the King raised his banner at Nottingham, and during the English Civil War London took the side of the parliament. Initially the king had the upper hand in military terms and in November he won the Battle of Brentford a few miles to the west of London. The City organized a new makeshift army and Charles hesitated and retreated. Subsequently an extensive system of fortifications was built to protect London from a renewed attack by the Royalists. This comprised a strong earthen rampart, enhanced with bastions and redoubts. It was well beyond the City walls and encompassed the whole urban area, including Westminster and Southwark. London was not seriously threatened by the royalists again, and the financial resources of the City made an important contribution to the parliamentarians' victory in the war.

The unsanitary and overcrowded City of London has suffered from the numerous outbreaks of the plague many times over the centuries, but in Britain it is the last major outbreak which is remembered as the "Great Plague" It occurred in 1665 and 1666 and killed around 60,000 people, which was one fifth of the population. The Great Plague was immediately followed by another catastrophe. In 1666 the Great Fire of London broke out at a bakery in Pudding Lane. The Monument was built to commemorate the fire. The fire destroyed about 60% of the City, including Old St Paul's Cathedral, 87 parish churches, 44 livery company halls and the Royal Exchange.

In the City itself there was a move from wooden buildings to stone and brick construction to reduce the risk of fire. Parliament's Rebuilding of London Act 1666 stated "building with brick [is] not only more comely and durable, but also safer against future perils of fire". From then on only door cases, window-frames and shop fronts were allowed to be made of wood. The rebuilt city generally followed the street plan of the old one, and most of it has survived into the 21st century. Nonetheless, the new City was different from the old one.

In 1700 London handled 80% of England's imports, 69% of its exports and 86% of its re-exports. Many of the goods were luxuries from the Americas and Asia such as silk, sugar, tea and tobacco.

The 18th century was a period of rapid growth for London, reflecting an increasing national population, the early stirrings of the Industrial Revolution, and London's role at the centre of the evolving British Empire.

In 1707 an Act of Union was passed merging the Scottish and the English Parliaments, thus establishing the Kingdom of Great Britain. A year later, in 1708 Christopher Wren's masterpiece, St Paul's Cathedral was completed on his birthday. However, the first service had been held on 2 December 1697;

Photo Credit 17:"St Paul's from the south-east with the tower of the destroyed Church of St Augustine to the right" by Nikopol Licensed under CC BY-SA 3.0 via Wikimedia Commons

more than 10 years earlier. This Cathedral replaced the original St. Paul's which had been completely destroyed in the Great Fire of

London. This building is considered one of the finest in Britain and a fine example of Baroque architecture.

During the Georgian period London spread beyond its traditional limits at an accelerating pace. In 1762 George III acquired Buckingham Palace (then called Buckingham House) from the Duke of Buckingham. It was enlarged over the next 75 years by architects such as John Nash.

A phenomenon of 18th-century London was the coffeehouse, which became a popular place to debate ideas. Growing literacy and the development of the printing press meant that news became widely available. Fleet Street became the centre of the embryonic British press during the century.

18th-century London was dogged by crime; the Bow Street Runners were established in 1750 as a professional police force. Penalties for crime were harsh, with the death penalty being applied for fairly minor crimes. Public hangings were common in London, and were popular public events.

Up until 1750, London Bridge was the only crossing over the Thames, but in that year Westminster Bridge was opened and, for the first time in history, London Bridge, in a sense, had a rival.

Photo Credit 18:"The first Westminster Bridge as painted by Canaletto, 1746" by Canaletto Licensed under Public Domain via Wikimedia Commons

entury saw the breakaway of the American colonies and many other unfortunate events in London, but also great change and Enlightenment. This all led into the beginning of modern times, the 19th century.

During the 19th century, London was transformed into the world's largest city and capital of the British Empire. Its population expanded from 1 million in 1800 to 6.7 million a century later. During this period, London became a global political, financial, and trading capital. In this position, it was largely unrivalled until the latter part of the century, when Paris and New York began to threaten its dominance.

19th-century London was transformed by the coming of the railways. A new network of metropolitan railways allowed for the development of suburbs in neighboring counties from which middle-class and wealthy people could commute to the centre. While this spurred the massive outward growth of the city, the growth of greater London also exacerbated the class divide, as the wealthier classes emigrated to the suburbs, leaving the poor to inhabit the inner city areas.

The first railway to be built in London was a line from London Bridge to Greenwich, which opened in 1836. This was soon followed by the opening of great rail termini which linked London to every corner of Brita

Photo Credit 19:"An early print of Euston showing the wrought iron roof of 1837"
Licensed under Public Domain via Wikimedia Commons

in. These included Euston station (1837), Paddington station (1838), Fenchurch Street station (1841), Waterloo station (1848), King's Cross station (1850), and St Pancras station (1863). From 1863, the first lines of the London Underground were constructed.

Towards the middle of the century, London's antiquated local government system, consisting of ancient parishes and vestries, struggled to cope with the rapid growth in population. In 1855 the Metropolitan Board of Works (MBW) was created to provide London with adequate infrastructure to cope with its growth. One of its first tasks was addressing London's sanitation problems. At the time, raw sewage was pumped straight into the River Thames. This culminated in The Great Stink of 1858. Parliament finally gave consent for the MBW to construc

t a large system of sewers. The engineer put in charge of building the new system was Joseph Bazalgette. When the London sewerage system was completed, the death toll in London dropped dramatically, and epidemics of cholera and other diseases were curtailed. Bazalgette's system is still in use today.[23]

One of the most famous events of 19th-century London was the Great Exhibition of 1851. Held at The Crystal Palace, the fair attracted 6 million visitors from across the world and displayed Britain at the height of its Imperial dominance.

In 1888, the new County of London was established, administered by the London County Council. This was the first elected London-wide administrative body, replacing the earlier Metropolitan Board of Works, which had been made up of appointees. The County of London covered broadly what was then the full extent of the London conurbation, although the conurbation later outgrew the boundaries of the county. In 1900, the county was sub-divided into 28 metropolitan boroughs, which formed a more local tier of administration than the county council.

Many famous buildings and landmarks of London were constructed during the 19th century including Trafalgar Square, Big Ben and the Houses of Parliament, The Royal Albert Hall, The Victoria and Albert Museum and Tower Bridge. London's population continued to grow rapidly in the early decades of the century, and public transport was greatly expanded. A large tram network was constructed by the London County Council. Improvements to London's overground and underground rail network, including large scale electrification were progressively carried out.

During World War I, London experienced its first bombing raids carried out by German zeppelin airships; these killed around 700 people and caused great terror, but were merely a foretaste of what was to come. The city of London would experience many

more terrors as a result of both World Wars. The largest explosion in London occurred during World War I: the Silvertown explosion, when a munitions factory containing 50 tons of TNT exploded, killing 73 and injuring 400.

The period between the two World Wars saw London's geographical extent growing more quickly than ever before or since. A preference for lower density suburban housing, typically semi-detached, by Londoners seeking a more "rural" lifestyle, superseded Londoners' old predilection for terraced houses. This was facilitated not only by a continuing expansion of the rail network, but also by slowly widening car ownership. London's suburbs expanded outside the boundaries of the County of London, into the neighboring counties of Essex, Hertfordshire, Kent, Middlesex and Surrey.

Like the rest of the country, London suffered severe unemployment during the Great Depression of the 1930s. Large numbers of Jewish immigrants fleeing from Nazi Germany, settled in London during the 1930s, mostly in the East End.

D

uring World War II, London, as many other British cities, suffered severe damage, being bombed extensively by the Luftwaffe as a part of The Blitz. Prior to the bombing, hundreds of thousands of children in London were evacuated to the countryside to avoid the bombing. Civilians took shelter from the air raids in underground stations.

The heaviest bombing took place during The Blitz between September 7th 1940 and May 10th 1941. During this period, London was subjected to 71 separate raids receiving over 18,000 tons of high explosive. One raid in December 1940, which became known as the Second Great Fire of London saw a firestorm engulf much of the City of London and destroy many historic buildings.

Having failed to defeat Britain, Hitler turned his attention to the Eastern front and regular bombing raids ceased. They began again, but on a smaller scale with the "Little Blitz" in early 1944. Towards the end of the war, during 1944/45 London again came under heavy attack by pilotless V-1 flying bombs and V-2 rockets, which were fired from Nazi occupied Europe. These attacks only came to an end when their launch sites were captured by advancing Allied forces.

Three years after the war, the 1948 Summer Olympics were held at the original Wembley Stadium, at a time when the city had barely recovered from the war. London's rebuilding was slow to begin. However, in 1951 the Festival of Britain was held, which marked an increasing mood of optimism and forward looking.

Through the 19th and in the early half of the 20th century, Londoners used coal for heating their homes, which produced large amounts of smoke. In combination with climatic conditions this often caused a characteristic smog which made London known for its typical "London Fog". London was sometimes referred to as "The Smoke" because of this. In 1952 this culminated in the disastrous Great Smog of 1952 which lasted for five days and killed over 4,000 people. In response to this, the Clean Air Act 1956 was passed, mandating the creating of "smokeless zones"where the use of "smokeless" fuels was required.

Starting in the mid-1960s, and partly as a result of the success of such UK musicians as the Beatles and the Rolling Stones, London became a centre for the worldwide youth culture, exemplified by the Swinging London subculture which made Carnaby Street a household name of youth fashion around the world. London's role as a trendsetter for youth fashion was revived strongly in the 1980s during the new wave and punk eras. In the mid-1990s this was revived to some extent with the emergence of the Britpop era.

From the 1950s onwards London became home to a large number of immigrants, largely from Commonwealth countries such as Jamaica, India, Bangladesh, Pakistan, which dramatically changed the face of London, turning it into one of the most diverse cities in Europe. However, the integration of the new immigrants was not always easy. Racial tensions emerged in events such as the Brixton Riots in the early 1980s.

From the beginning of "The Troubles" in Northern Ireland in the early 1970s until the mid-1990s

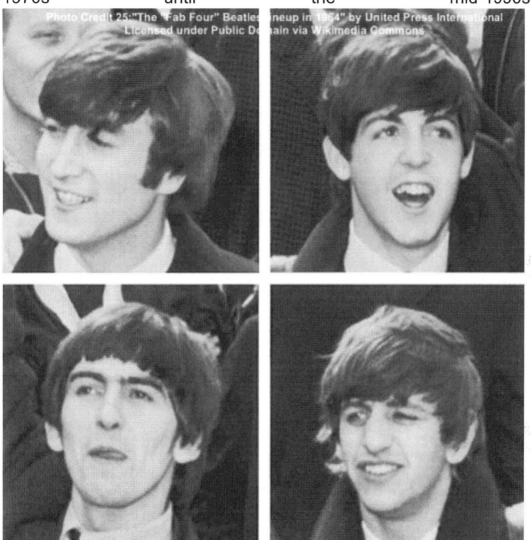

London was subjected to repeated terrorist attacks by the Provisional IRA.

The outward expansion of London was slowed by the war, and the introduction of the Metropolitan Green Belt. Due to this outward expansion, in 1965 the old County of London (which by now only covered part of the London conurbation) and the London County Council were abolished, and the much larger area of Greater London was established with a new Greater London Council (GLC) to administer it, along with 32 new London boroughs.

Greater London's population declined steadily in the decades after World War II, from an estimated peak of 8.6 million in 1939 to around 6.8 million in the 1980s. However, it then began to increase again in the late 1980s, encouraged by strong economic performance and an increasingly positive image.

London's traditional status as a major port declined dramatically in the post-war decades as the old Docklands could not accommodate large modern container ships. The principal ports for London moved downstream to the ports of Felixstowe and Tilbury. The docklands area had become largely derelict by the 1980s, but was redeveloped into flats and offices from the mid-1980s onwards. The Thames Barrier was completed in the 1980s to protect London against tidal surges from the North Sea.

In the early 1980s political disputes between the GLC run by Ken Livingstone and the Conservative government of Margaret Thatcher led to the GLC's abolition in 1986, with most of its powers relegated to the London boroughs. This left London as the only large metropolis in the world without a central administration.

In 2000, London-wide government was restored, with the creation of the Greater London Authority (GLA) by Tony Blair's government, covering the same area of Greater London. The new authority had similar powers to the old GLC, but was made up of a directly elected Mayor and a London Assembly. The first election took place on May 4th, with Ken Livingstone comfortably regaining his previous post. London was recognized as one of the nine regions of England. In global perspective, it was emerging as a World city widely compared to New York and Tokyo.

Around the start of the 21st century, London hosted the much derided Millennium Dome at Greenwich, to mark the new century. Other Millennium projects were more successful. One was the largest observation wheel in the world, the "Millennium Wheel", or the London Eye, which was erected as a temporary structure, but soon became a fixture, and draws four million visitors a year. The National Lottery also released a flood of funds for major enhancements to existing attractions, for example the roofing of the Great Court at the British Museum.

On 6 July 2005 London won the right to host the 2012 Olympics and Paralympics making it the first city to host the modern games three times. However, celebrations were cut short the following day when the city was rocked by a series of terrorist attacks. More than 50 were killed and 750 injured in three bombings on London Underground trains and a fourth on a double decker bus near King's Cross.

In the public there was ambivalence leading-up to the Olympics, though public sentiment changed strongly in their favor following a successful opening ceremony and when the anticipated organizational and transport problems never occurred.London today is full of excellent bars, galleries, museums, parks and theatres. It is also the most culturally and ethnically diverse part of the country. In 1777, noted diarist Samuel Johnson famously said "When a man is tired of London he is tired of life." Whether you are interested in ancient history, modern art, opera or underground raves, London is a global centre of history, learning and culture.

Chapter 3: Getting Around

The best way to explore and move around London is its comprehensive public transportation system. Although sometimes unreliable, it is often the fastest option to get from one point to another.

Transport for London (TfL) is a government organization responsible for all public transport. Their website contains maps and all info you need to know to move around. TfL publishes a useful 'coping guide' specially designed for travellers who wish to use public transport during their visit to London. They also offer a 24-hour travel information line for suggestions on getting from A to B, and for up to the minute information on how services are running.

the number of paper tickets. Usage is encouraged by offering substantially cheaper fares than with cash though the acceptance of cash is being phased out. On London buses, cash is no longer accepted.

There is a single ticketing system, called Oyster, which enables travellers to switch between modes of transport on one ticket. A standard Oyster card is a blue credit-card-sized stored-value contactless smartcard that can hold single tickets, period tickets and travel permits, which must be added to the card before travel. Passengers touch it on an electronic reader when entering and leaving the transport system in order to validate it or deduct funds. Cards may be "topped-up" by recurring payment authority, by online purchase, at credit card terminals or by cash, the last two methods at stations or ticket offices. The card is designed to reduce the number of transactions at ticket offices and

As part of TfL's 'Future Ticketing Program, the Oyster card platform is due to be replaced by a contactless payment card system, the first stage of which is due to be completed by June 2015. On June 8th 2015, TfL confirmed that it would start accepting Apple Pay as another form of fare payment on its network from July 2015.

Oyster cards can be purchased from a number of different outlets in the London area; London Underground or London Overground ticket windows, ticket machines at London Underground stations, which accept banknotes, coins, and credit and debit cards. There are around 4,000 Oyster Ticket Stop agents (usually newsagent's shops), selected National Rail stations, some of which are also served by London Underground, Travel Information Centers, online via the TfL website or by telephone sales from TfL.

Visitor Oyster cards can be obtained from Visit Britain outlets around the world, and from other transport operators, such as EasyJet and Gatwick Express, and online and from any ticket office. A £5 deposit is required which will be refunded in cash upon return of the card. Any remaining credit on the card is refundable as well.

Ticket vending machines on most National Rail stations will top-up Oyster cards and sell tickets that can be loaded on to Oyster. New Oyster cards are not available at most National Rail stations and termini.

An Oyster card can hold up to three season tickets at the same time. Season tickets are Bus & Tram Passes or Travelcards lasting 7 days, 1-month, or any duration up to one year (annual).

There is no essential difference in validity or cost between a 7-day, monthly or longer period Travelcard on Oyster and one on a traditional paper ticket; they are valid on all Underground, Overground, DLR, bus, tram and national rail services within the zones purchased. A Travelcard entitles the holder to unlimited travel in Greater London on London Buses, Tramlink, London Underground, London Overground, Docklands Light Railway and National Rail services. Travelcards are issued for periods of one or seven days, or for any period from one month to one year. They provide travel within six numbered concentric zones.

Depending on where it is purchased, and the length of validity, a Travelcard is either printed on a paper ticket with a magnetic stripe or encoded onto an Oyster card, Transport for London's contactless electronic smart card. The cost of a Travelcard is determined by the area it covers.

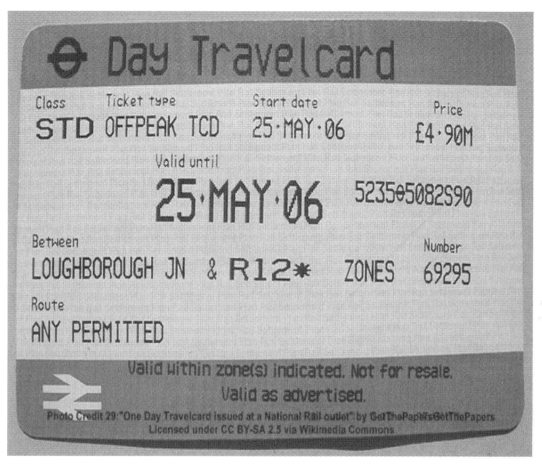

Although TfL asks all Oyster users to swipe their card at entry/exit points of their journey, in practice Travelcard holders only need to "touch in" and "touch out" to operate ticket barriers or because they intend to travel outside the zones for which their Travelcard is valid. As long as the Travelcard holder stays within their permitted zones no fare will be deducted from the pay as you go funds on the card. The Oyster system checks that the Travelcard is valid in the zones it is being used in.

In addition to holding Travelcards and bus passes, Oyster cards can also be used as stored-value cards, holding electronic funds of money. Amounts are deducted from the card each time it is used, and the funds can be "recharged" when required. The maximum value that an Oyster card may hold is £90. This system is known as "pay as you go" (abbreviated PAYG), because instead of holding a season ticket, the user only pays at the point of use.

It is possible to have a negative pay-as-you-go balance after completing a journey, but this will prevent the card from being used (even if it is loaded with a valid Travelcard) until the card is topped up.

When the PAYG balance runs low, the balance can be topped up at the normal sales points or ticket machines at London Underground or London Overground stations, Oyster Ticket Stops or some National Rail stations. All ticket offices at stations run by London Underground will sell or recharge Oyster cards, or handle Oyster card refunds. However, some Tube stations are actually operated by National Rail train operating companies, and their ticket offices will not deal with Oyster refunds. DLR does not have any ticket offices which sell any Oyster card top-ups or handle refunds, except for the information office at London City Airport.

To encourage passengers to switch to Oyster, cash fares are generally much more expensive than PAYG fares (including Bus and Tram fares). As of May 2015 the single Oyster fare for a bus journey is £1.50, but capped at £4.40 for any number of trips in a day (including trips by Tram and tube). Cash is no longer accepted on London's buses, but a contactless debit or credit card can be used in place of an Oyster card at the same fare. A single tram journey is charged as per a single bus journey, but the tram ticket machines do still accept cash (£2.40) for a single journey.

Using pay as you go, a single trip on the Tube within Zone 1 costs £2.30 (compared to £4.70 cash), or £1.70 at peak times (£1.50 off peak or £4.70 for cash at any time) within any other single zone. Journeys in multiple zones are progressively more expensive.

The Oyster pay as you go system coupled with the zoned fare system inevitably gives rise to some quirks in the fares charged. A 9 stop journey between Clapham Junction and West Hampstead on the overground is charged at £1.70 at peak times (£1.50 off peak) whereas a 1 stop journey between Shoreditch High Street and Whitechapel on the same line costs £2.30 at all times. This occurs because Shoreditch High Street is the only station on the line exclusively in zone 1, all others being in zone 2.

In order to prevent "misuse" by a stated 2% of passengers, from 19 November 2006 pay as you go users who do not both 'touch in' at the start and 'touch out' at the end of their rail network journeys are charged a "maximum Oyster fare"– up to £7.20 (presumably depending on whether journeys have been made during or outside peak times) for most journeys, or more if the journey begins or ends at certain National Rail stations. Depending on the journey made, the difference between this maximum fare and the actual fare due is automatically refunded to the user's Oyster card upon touching out.

Users must touch in and out even if the ticket barriers are open. At stations where Oyster is accepted but that do not have ticket barriers, an Oyster validator will be provided for the purposes of touching in and out. The maximum Oyster fare applies even if the daily price cap has been reached and does not count towards the cap. When using the Tube, you'll notice that many stations in London are very close together but you cannot transfer between train lines within the ticket barriers. This is because historically the train lines were built by competing companies and there was no traveller need, or commercial reason to create interchanges back then. Now we have OSI (Outside Stat

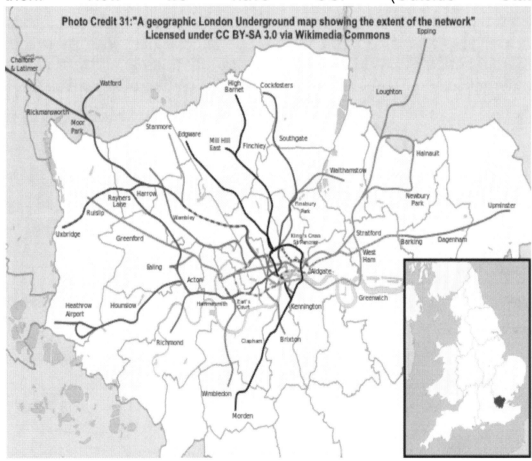

Photo Credit 31:"A geographic London Underground map showing the extent of the network" Licensed under CC BY-SA 3.0 via Wikimedia Commons

ion Interchange), this means that you can touch your oyster card out of a station, walk the 5 minutes to a nearby station and touch in again, without charging you two tickets - you will be charged as if you made an interchange without leaving the station. This is also the case at some large stations which are integrated, but it might be easier to touch out at one entrance and touch back in again at another entrance when changing lines, such as transferring between the Northern and Circle, H&C or Metropolitan lines at King's Cross St. Pancras station. Be warned that there is a time limit of how long you can stay out of the network before your touch-in is considered a new journey.

The main source of public transport in London revolves around the Underground (or the Tube as it is known to Londoners). This extensive network of 12 lines can get you to most places in the centre of the city quickly. Delays on the Tube are not uncommon, so look out for service updates immediately beyond the ticket barriers at most stations or listen for announcements on the platforms. However, even with a delay here or there, the Tube is often the fastest way to cover a large amount of ground.

Trains and platforms are described as Eastbound, Westbound, Northbound or Southbound depending on the direction of the line and the station. However, be sure to confirm that the direction of the train more or less coincides with your destination. The front of the train, and the platform indicator, will show the ultimate destination of the train which is usually (though not always) the last station on the line. It can still be confusing until you get the hang of it all, but don't despair, help is at hand: Tube staff is knowledgeable about the system and can always be found at station ticket barriers and also on most platforms. Also, most platforms have white circular Help Points from which you can contact a central information point. Press the green button to report an emergency and the blue button for general queries. At some stations the Help Point also has a red fire alarm that you should use if you spot a fire. It's also very helpful to pick up one of the free maps available at all train station ticket offices. Each line has its own unique color so it's easy to identify each line on maps and signs throughout the system. Similar maps in a variety of languages can also be found online.

The Tube maps on the station walls are diagrammatic representations of the routes and are drawn so that they are easy to read: they do not provide an accurate depiction of the physical location of the stations. Thus, even though you would not be able to determine it from the official Underground map, some tube stations are within easy walking distance of each other. Knowing this can be useful if you know that where you are going is near a particular tube station: it could save you an unnecessary change onto another line with the attendant waste of time.

Here's a list of stations within walking distance of each other; Paddington (B, Ci, Di, H) - Lancaster Gate (Ce); Great Portland Street (H, Ci, M) - Regent's Park (B); Great Portland Street (H, Ci, M) - Warren Street (N, V); Great Portland Street (H, Ci, M) - Goodge Street (N); Warren Street (N, V) - Euston Square (H, Ci, M); Euston (N, V) - Euston Square (H, Ci, M); Bayswater (Ci, D) - Queensway (Ce); Tottenham Court Road (Ce) - Covent Garden (P); Farringon (H, Ci, M) - Chancery Lane (Ce); Cannon Street (Ci, Di) - Bank (Ce, N, W, DLR); Cannon Street (Ci, Di) - St Paul's (Ce); Mansion House (Ci, Di) - St Paul's (Ce) and Blackfriars (Ci, Di) - St Paul's (Ce).

The letters in parentheses are the lines: B - Bakerloo, Ce - Central, Ci - Circle, Di - District, DLR - Docklands Light Railway, H - Hammersmith & City, M - Metropolitan, N - Northern, P - Piccadilly, V – Victoria and W - Waterloo & City.

On hot days it is also advisable to take a bottle of water with you as Underground trains are not air-conditioned. During particularly hot spells of weather water is sometimes handed out on the Underground. Delays seem to also happen more often during the summer   and   can   make   this   situati

Photo Credit 32:"Lancaster Gate tube" by Tom Page
Licensed under CC BY-SA 2.0 via Wikimedia Commons

on worse if you haven't brought some water to help keep you cool and hydrated.

Last trains leave central London at around 00:30 weekdays, 23:30 Sundays.   First trains leave the suburbs around 05:00. Check the TfL Journey Planner to establish if you can make the trip by Tube when travelling early or late. Finally, if you are travelling with a group of up to five and it's not rush hour, you might find that a taxi doesn't cost much more than the Tube would cost for the lot of you, and it can be much quicker, for short trips.

The Underground is experiencing a phenomenal program of repair, refurbishment and modernization work. This is the oldest and one of the most extensive subway systems in the world, and following some years of under investment by governments of all political persuasions it has finally been recognized that things wear out and need fixing. Unfortunately, for long-term gain this means short-term pain and some stations, station facilities (escalators/lifts etc.) and sections of lines may be out of service at various times, especially weekends and/or late evenings/early mornings.

All these planned closures are well publicized, look for posters and leaflets at stations and listen for announcements over the PA systems on trains and stations. Better still, check whether the route you want to take is affected before you travel by visiting the dedicated section of their website; check before you travel by using the TfL Journey Planner, which also works for bus, tram, DLR, river and some suburban rail routes.

Outside of the centre of London, Tube stations are farther apart, so buses help fill the gaps. Also, the budget-conscious will find that the bus offers a cheaper alternative, even if it is a slower journey.

The bus stops are well signposted and each stop gives information about all the bus destinations, alternative stops nearby f

Photo Credit 33: "An example of a typical London bus stop" by Panhard Licensed under CC BY 2.5 via Wikimedia Commons

or other buses, frequency, etc. On most routes buses are frequent during normal Monday-Friday daytime hours, with them becoming less frequent early morning, late evening and weekends.

Do note that in very busy areas serviced by many buses - like Oxford Street - not all buses stop at the same places. Each stop will have a large sign showing on a map where all the various buses stop. While the tourist mantra that "all buses eventually go to Trafalgar Square" is not quite true, the entire city is well covered by bus routes and most trips can be completed with no more than one change.

If using the buses the spider maps are especially useful as they give complete details for each major bus stop. It is helpful to find the closest stop to your hotel and to print out that spider map before you begin your trip. The only tricky bit is that the overview map is very short of detail and the novice traveller will need to click on several options before finding which bit of London matches their location. If your hotel is a bit away from a Tube station, be sure to find the information on a bus route that takes you to the Tube.

But other than that, you're not likely to be able to have information on all the bus routes in advance. You can always try finding a stop near wherever you happen to be, and reading the information there.

On regular buses, only board via the front door and either show your ticket or pass to the driver, touch your Oyster or Contactless card on the reader. On "new routemaster" buses you may board any of the three doors if using Oyster or Contactless. If using a paper travelcard you must board at the front and show your ticket to the driver. There are Oyster readers at each door.

To experience the "heritage routes", ride on an old Routemaster red London bus, a design icon synonymous with London, use the 15 from Trafalgar Square to Tower Hill. Standard fares apply on the historic route. Bus Passes, Travelcards, Freedom Passes, and Oyster cards are accepted - but contactless bank cards are not. Traditional Routemaster buses have taken out of public service from all other routes, though the "New Routemaster" now operates on many routes in central London. Traditional Routemasters are used by several private companies for London tours and entertainment but at a price.

Night buses cover the whole of the London and generally run all through the night at frequencies ranging from hourly to 4 an hour, seven nights a week. The most densely trafficked routes are the radial ones from the centre out into the suburbs and vice versa. Those that follow exactly the same route as their daytime equivalents carry the same route numbers. However, some differ from the daytime routes. These can be recognized by the prefix 'N' in front of the route number. Check the times and the route detail on notices at the bus stops.

You can think of the Docklands Light Railway (DLR) and the Tramlink as extensions of the U

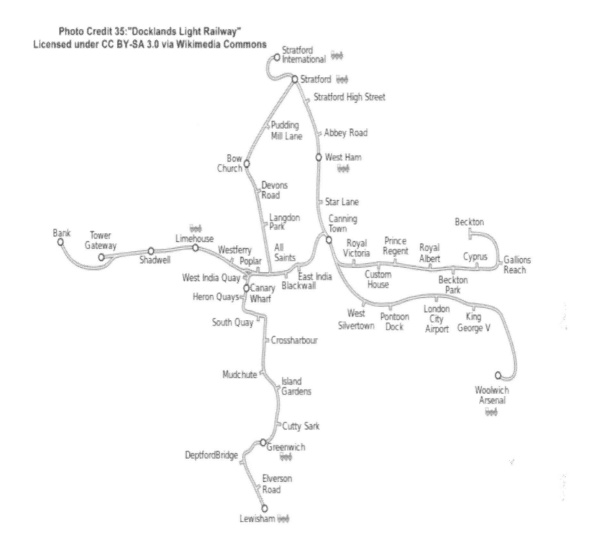

nderground. Travelcards purchased at Tube Stations will be valid on the DLR and Tramlink.

The DLR is the easiest way to reach a number of attractions in East London. The DLR connects with a number of the other train services (including connections at Tower Hill or Bank Stations) and can be used to reach Greenwich, Canary Wharf, and Stratford.

The TramLink runs across South London with three routes. The first takes you across South London starting at Wimbledon with many connections to the National Rail System. The ride from Wimbledon to Croydon takes approximately 25 minutes, then carries on to New Addington arriving about 15 minutes later. The second route goes from Croydon to Beckenham J

unction taking about 22 minutes. The third route runs from Croydon to Elmers End and takes about 15 minutes. TramLink is considered part of the bus network so a Travelcard or bus pass is valid regardless of zones.

There are a number of different routes along the River Thames. The faster commuter services operate all day from Greenwich Pier to Embankment and from Putney and Chelsea Harbor to Blackfriars during Peak Hours only. These routes will pass a number of places of interest including the Houses of Parliament and London Bridge. A return fare from Putney to Blackfriars will cost approximately £12.

There are also a number of leisure cruises available. The length of time it takes on a number of routes means that you should consider them an attraction in their own right rather than as just a means to get from one place to another. The journey along the River Thames, once out of the City, gives you the chance to view a number of the Riverside towns and a chance to see a large variety of birds and other wildlife that live on the banks of the River Thames. Most leisure services will also have toilet facilities and light snacks and drink available (although these can be expensive so plan ahead and bring   your   ow

n). A number of routes will only make a couple of round trips each day so it important to get hold of the timetable and plan your trip in advance. The timetable will also vary depending on tides, weather conditions, and season which is another good reason to plan ahead as much as possible.

Fares for River Services vary a great deal between routes (and provider). Travelcards will get you a discount off the price of the Riverboat services if you show your Travelcard at the time of purchasing your ticket (this discount is currently 1/3 off the price). You can also purchase DLR Rail and River Rover tickets (around £9) which combine travel on the DLR with hop-on, hop-off travel on City Cruises riverboats between Westminster, Waterloo, Tower and Greenwich Piers. You should try to purchase your ticket from the ticket office prior to boarding the boat at the pier where you are stating your journey. However on some services you will need to buy your ticket on the boat so don't worry if you can't find a ticket office or if it's closed.

Once you leave Central London or if you are travelling south of the River Thames, the best public transport option will often be National Rail. There are numerous connections to the Rail System from the Tube. Travelcards can be used for travel on the National Rail (but not the Heathrow Express). Single and Return Fares are also available. Oyster cards can be used up to Zone 6 except certain services including Heathrow Express, Heathrow Connect and HS1.

There are a number of attractions within Central London that also require you to transfer to a National Rail Train as no underground station is available. Attractions within London that have an "national rail" station only a short walk away include Buckingham Palace, The National Gallery, The Tower of London, and the London Aquarium. The easiest way to access Hampton Court Palace will be the South West Trains which runs directly from London Waterloo to Hampton Court (although the journey by Riverboat can also be a good option if you have the time).

Complete information on the London transport system can be found on the Transport for London website. This site also provides a Journey Planner which can be useful, although it might not always bring up the best route. London has two types of taxis: the famous black cab, and so-called minicabs. Black cabs are the only ones licensed to 'ply for hire' (pick people up off the street), while minicabs are more accurately described as 'private hire vehicles' and need to be pre-booked. The famous black cab of London (not always black!) can be hailed from the curb or found at one of the many designated taxi ranks. It is possible to book black cabs by phone, for a fee, but if you are in central London it will usually be quicker to hail one from the street. Their amber TAXI light will be on if they are available. Drivers must pass a rigorous exam of central London's streets, known as 'The Knowledge', in order to be licensed to drive a black cab. This means they can supposedly navigate you to almost any London street without reference to a map. They are a cheap transport option if there are five passengers as they do not charge extras, and many view them as an essential experience for any visitor to London. Black cabs charge by distance and by the minute, are non-smoking, and have a minimum charge of £2.40. Tipping is not mandatory in either taxis or minicabs, but it's welcome. Londoners will often just round up to the nearest pound. Taxis are required by law to take you up to 12 miles or up to one hour duration, if the destination is in Greater London (20 miles if starting at Heathrow Airport) if their TAXI light is on when you hail them, unless they have a good reason. However some, especially older drivers, dislike leaving the centre of town, or going south of the River Thames. A good way to combat being left at the side of the curb is to open the back door, or even get into the cab, before stating your destination.

Minicabs are normal cars which are licensed hire vehicles that you need to book by phone or at a minicab office. They generally charge a fixed fare for a journey, best agreed before you get in the car. Minicabs are sometimes cheaper than black cabs, although this

is not necessarily the case for short journeys. Minicabs can be significantly cheaper for airport journeys - for example, a minicab from Heathrow to South-West London will cost around £36, whereas a black cab will cost over £100. Drivers are not tested as rigorously as black cab drivers, so they will typically not speak English very well and rely on a GPS to find their way, but will still get you from A to B. Licensed minicabs display a Transport For London (TFL) License Plate - usually in the front window. One of the features of the license plate is a blue version of the famous London Underground "roundel". A list of licensed minicab operators can be found at TfL Findaride.

Note that some areas in London are poorly serviced by black cabs, particularly late at night. This has led to a large number of illegal minicabs operating - just opportunistic people, with a car, looking to make some fast money. Some of these operators can be fairly aggressive in their attempts to find customers, and it's now barely possible to walk late at night through any part of London with a modicum of nightlife without being approached. You should avoid mini-cabs touting for business off the street or outside nightclubs and either take a black cab, book a licensed minicab by telephone, or take a night bus. These ill

Photo Credit 39:"Private hire minicabs" by Walter Baxter
Licensed under CC BY-SA 2.0 via Wikimedia Commons

egal drivers are unlicensed and sadly they are often unsafe: a number of women are assaulted every week by illegal minicab operators (on average 11 reported per month).

Chapter 4: London's Most Famous Attractions

London is home to 4 World Heritage Sites. The first one is Her Majesty's Royal Palace and Fortress, known as the Tower of London. It's a historic castle located on the north bank of the River Thames in central London. It lies within the London Borough of Tower Hamlets, separated from the eastern edge of the square mile of the City of London by the op

en space known as Tower Hill.

It was founded towards the end of 1066 as part of the Norman Conquest of England. The White Tower, which gives the entire castle its name, was built by William the Conqueror in 1078, and was a resented symbol of oppression, inflicted upon London by the new ruling elite. The castle was used as a prison from 1100 until 1952, although that was not its primary purpose.

The Tower of London has played a prominent role in English history. It was besieged several times and controlling it has been important to controlling the country. The Tower has served variously as an armory, a treasury, a menagerie, the home of the Royal Mint, a public records office, and the home of the Crown Jewels of England. From the early 14th century until the reign of Charles II, a procession would be led from the Tower to Westminster Abbey on the coronation of a monarch. In the absence of the monarch, the Constable of the Tower is in charge of the castle. This was a powerful and trusted position in the medieval period. In the late 15th century the castle was the prison of the Princes in the Tower. Under the Tudors, the Tower became used less as a royal residence, and despite attempts to refortify and repair the castle its defenses lagged behind developments to deal with artillery. The peak period of the castle's use as a prison was the 16th and 17th centuries, when many figures who had fallen into disgrace, such as Elizabeth I before she became queen, were held within its walls. This use has led to the phrase "sent to the Tower".

The Tower of London has become established as one of the most popular tourist attractions in the country. It has been a tourist attraction since at least the Elizabethan period, when it was one of the sights of London that foreign visitors wrote about. Its most popular attractions were the Royal Menagerie and displays of armor. The Crown Jewels also garner much interest, and have been on public display since 1669. The Tower steadily gained popularity with tourists through the 19th century, despite the opposition of the Duke of Wellington to visitors. Numbers became so high that by 1851 a purpose-built ticket office was erected. By the end of the century, over 500,000 were visiting the castle every year.

In the 21st century tourism is the Tower's primary role. However, the Tower is still home to the ceremonial regimental headquarters of the Royal Regiment of Fusiliers, and the museum dedicated to it and its predecessor,   th

e Royal Fusiliers. Also, a detachment of the unit providing the Queen's Guard at Buckingham Palace still mounts a guard at the Tower, and with the Yeomen Warders, takes part in the Ceremony of the Keys each day. On several occasions through the year gun salutes are fired from the Tower by the Honorable Artillery Company, these consist of 62 rounds for royal occasions, and 41 on other occasions.

The Tower of London is cared for by an independent charity, Historic Royal Palaces, which receives no funding from the Government or the Crown. In 1988, the Tower of London was added to the UNESCO list of World Heritage Sites, in recognition of its global importance and to help conserve and protect the site. However, recent developments, such as the construction of skyscrapers nearby, have pushed the Tower towards being added to the United Nations' Heritage in Danger List.

The remains of the medieval palace have been open to the public since 2006. Visitors can explore the chambers restored to their former glory, once used by past kings and queens. At least six ravens are kept at the Tower at all times, in accordance with the belief that if they are absent, the kingdom will fall. They are under the care of the Yeomen Warders. The earliest known reference to a Tower raven is a picture from 1883. As well as having ceremonial duties, the Yeoman Warders provide guided tours around the Tower.

To get there use the Tube, nearest station is Tower Hill. Use District or Circle lines to Tower Hill station. Follow direction signs to the Tower. The main entrance is a 5 minute walk from the station. DLR's Tower Gateway Station is located adjacent to Tower Hill station. Follow direction signs to the main entrance of the Tower. Bus routes 15, 42, 78, 100, RV1 also serve the Tower, as well as all major sightseeing bus tours.

The Royal Botanic Gardens at Kew, another World Heritage Site, is the world's largest collection of living plants. It was founded in 1840 from the exotic garden at Kew Park in the London Borough of Richmond upon Thames. Its living collections include more than 30,000 different kinds of plants, while the herbarium, which is one of the largest in the world, has over seven million preserved plant specimens. The library contains more than 750,000 volumes, and the illustrations collection contains more than 175,000 prints and drawings of plants. It is one of London's top tourist attractions. In 2003, the gardens were put on the UNESCO list of World Heritage Sites.

Kew Gardens, together with the botanic gardens at Wakehurst Place in Sussex, are managed by the Royal Botanic Gardens. Kew (brand name Kew), is an internationally important botanical research and education institution that employs 750 people, and is a non-departmental public body sponsored by the Department for Environment, Food and Rural Affairs.

The Kew site consists of 121 hectares of gardens and botanical glasshouses, four Grade I listed buildings and 36 Grade II listed structures, all set in an internationally significant landscape.

Kew Gardens is accessible by a number of gates. Currently, there are four gates into Kew Gardens that are open to the public: the Elizabeth Gate, which is situated at the west end of Kew Green, and was originally called the Main Gate before being renamed in 2012 to commemorate the Diamond Jubilee of Elizabeth II; the Brentford Gate, which faces the River Thames; the Victoria Gate (named after Queen Victoria), situated in Kew Road, which is also the location of the Visitors' Centre; and the Lion Gate, also situated in Kew Road.

Kew Gardens station, a London Underground and National Rail station opened in 1869

Photo Credit 42:"Kew Gardens Palm House" by Diliff Licensed under CC BY-SA 3.0 via Wikimedia Commons

and served by both the District line and the London Overground services on the North London Line, is the nearest train station to the gardens – only 400 meters along Lichfield Road from the Victoria Gate entrance. Built by the London and South Western Railway, the English Heritage listed building is one of the few remaining original 19th-century stations on the North London Line, and the only station on the London Underground with a pub on the platform.

Kew Bridge station, on the other side of the Thames, 800 meters from the Elizabeth Gate entrance via Kew Bridge, is served by South West Trains from Clapham Junction and Waterloo. London Buses route 65, between Ealing Broadway and Kingston, stops near the Lion Gate and Victoria Gate entrances; route 391, between Fulham and Richmond, stops near Kew Gardens station; while routes 237 and 267 stop at Kew Bridge station. The Palace of Westminster is the meeting place of the House of Commons and the House of Lords, the two houses of the Parliament of th

Photo Credit 43:"The Palace of Westminster with Elizabeth Tower and Westminster Bridge" by Mgimelfarb
Licensed under Public Domain via Wikimedia Commons

e United Kingdom. Commonly known as the Houses of Parliament after its occupants, the Palace lies on the northern bank of the River Thames in the City of Westminster, in central London. Its name, which derives from the neighboring Westminster Abbey, may refer to either of two structures: the Old Palace, a medieval building complex that was destroyed by fire in 1834, and its replacement, the New Palace that stands today. For ceremonial purposes, the palace retains its original style and status as a royal residence and is the property of the Crown.

The first royal palace was built on the site in the eleventh century, and Westminster was the primary residence of the Kings of England until a fire destroyed much of the complex in 1512. After that, it served as the home of the Parliament of England, which had been meeting there since the thirteenth century, and also as the seat of the Royal Courts of Justice, based in and around Westminster Hall. In 1834, an even greater fire ravaged the heavily rebuilt Houses of Parliament, and the only medieval structures of significance to survive were Westminster Hall, the Cloisters of St Stephen's, the Chapel of St Mary Undercroft, and the Jewel Tower. The remains of the Old Palace (with the exception of the detached Jewel Tower) were incorporated into its much larger replacement, which contains over 1,100 rooms organized symmetrically around two series of courtyards. Part of the New Palace's area of 3.24 hectares was reclaimed from the Thames, which is the setting of its principal 266-metre façade, called the River Front.

Construction started in 1840 and lasted for thirty years, suffering great delays and cost overruns; works for the interior decoration continued intermittently well into the twentieth century. Major conservation work has been carried out since, to reverse the effects of London's air pollution, and extensive repairs took place after the Second World War, including the reconstruction of the Commons Chamber following its bombing in 1941.

The Palace is one of the centers of political life in the United Kingdom; "Westminster" has become a metonym for the UK

Parliament, and the Westminster system of government has taken its name after it.

Free guided tours of the Palace are held throughout the parliamentary session for UK residents, who can apply through their MP or a member of the House of Lords. The tours last about 75 minutes and include the state rooms, the chambers of the two Houses and Westminster Hall. Paid-for tours are available to both UK and overseas visitors during the summer recess. UK residents may also tour the Elizabeth Tower, by applying through their local Member of Parliament; overseas visitors and small children are not allowed.

The exterior of the Palace of Westminster—especially the clock tower which houses the bell known as Big Ben, and its setting on the bank of the River Thames—is recognized worldwide, and is one of the most visited tourist attractions in London. The United Nations Educational, Scientific and Cultural Organization (UNESCO) classifies the Palace of Westminster, along with neighboring Westminster Abbey and St Margaret's, as a World Heritage Site. It is also a Grade I listed building.

Big Ben is the nickname for the Great Bell of the clock at the north end of the Palace of Westminster in London, and often extended to refer to the clock and the clock tower. The tower is officially known as the Elizabeth Tower, renamed as such to celebrate the Diamond Jubilee of Elizabeth II. The tower holds the second largest four-faced chiming clock in the world. The tower was completed in 1858 and had its 150th anniversary on 31 May 2009.

Westminster Abbey, formally titled the Collegiate Church of St Peter at Westminster, is a large, mainly Gothic abbey church in the City of Westminster, located just to the west of the Palace of Westminster. It is one of the most notable religious buildings in the United Kingdom and has been the traditional place of coronation and burial site for English and, later, British monarchs. Between 1540 and 1556 the abbey had the status of a cathedral. Since 1560, however, the building is no longer an abbey nor a cathedral, having instead the status of a "Royal Peculiar"– a church responsible directly to the Sovereign. The building itself is the original abbey church.

According to a tradition first reported by Sulcard in about 1080, a church was founded at the site (then known as Thorn Ey) in th

e 7th century, at the time of Mellitus, a Bishop of London. Construction of the present church began in 1245, on the orders of Henry III. Since 1066, when Harold Godwinson and William the Conqueror were crowned, the coronations of English and British monarchs have been held here. Since 1100, there have been at least 16 royal weddings at the abbey.

The church of St Margaret is situated in the grounds of Westminster Abbey on Parliament Square, and is the Anglican parish church of the House of Commons of the United Kingdom in London. It is dedicated to Margaret of Antioch.

It was originally founded in the twelfth century by Benedictine monks, so that local people who lived in the area around the Abbey could worship separately at their own simpler parish church. St Margaret's was rebuilt from 1486 to 1523. It became the parish church of the Palace of Westminster in 1614, when

the Puritans of the seventeenth century, unhappy with the highly liturgical Abbey, chose to hold Parliamentary services in the more "suitable" St Margaret's.

The north-west tower was rebuilt by John James from 1734 to 1738; at the same time, the whole structure was encased in Portland stone. Both the eastern and the western porch were added later by J. L. Pearson. The church's interior was greatly restored and altered to its current appearance by Sir George Gilbert Scott in 1877, although many of the Tudor features were retained.

The nearest London Underground station is Westminster, on the District, Circle and Jubilee lines.

In 1997, Maritime Greenwich was added to the list of World Heritage Sites, for the concentration and quality of buildings of historic and architectural interest. These can be divided into the group of buildings along the riverfront, Greenwich Park and the Georgian and Victorian town centre. In recognition of the suburb's astronomical links,   Asteroid   2830   h

Photo Credit 46:"The church of St Margaret" Licensed under CC BY-SA 3.0 via Wikimedia Commons

as   been named 'Greenwich'.

The Discover Greenwich Visitor Centre provides an introduction to the history and attractions in the Greenwich World Heritage Site. It is located in the Pepys Buildings near to the Cutty Sark within the grounds of the Old Royal Naval College, (formerly Greenwich Hospital). The centre opened in March 2010, and admission is free.

Greenwich is notable for its maritime history and for giving its name to the Greenwich Meridian (0° longitude) and Greenwich Mean Time. The town became the site of a royal palace, the Palace of Placentia from the 15th century, and was the birthplace of many Tudors, including Henry VIII and Elizabeth I. The palace fell into disrepair during the English Civil War and was rebuilt as the Royal Naval Hospital for Sailors by Sir Christopher Wren and his assistant Nicholas Hawksmoor. These buildings became the Royal Naval College in 1873, and they remained an establishment for military education until 1998 when they passed into the hands of the Greenwich Foundation. The historic rooms within these buildings remain open to the public; other buildings are used by University of Greenwich and Trinity Laban Conservatoire of Music and Dance.

The town became a popular resort in the 18th century and many grand houses were built there, such as Vanbrugh Castle (1717) established on Maze Hill, next to the park. From the Georgian period estates of houses were constructed above the town centre. The maritime connections of Greenwich were celebrated in the 20th century, with the siting of the Cutty Sark and Gipsy Moth IV next to the river front, and the National Maritime Museum in the former buildings of the Royal Hospital School in 1934. Greenwich formed part of Kent until 1889 when the County of London was created.

Greenwich is served by two rail stations, Greenwich station and Maze Hill station with services to London Cannon Street, Barnehurst, Dartford and Gillingham. Greenwich is also served by the Docklands Light Railway, with services from Greenwich station and Cutty Sark to Lewisham, Canary Wharf, Stratford and Bank.

Several Transport for London bus services link it with areas including Catford, Elephant and Castle, Eltham, Lewisham, Peckham, New Cross, Sidcup, Thamesmead, Waterloo and Woolwich.

Beside the 4 World Heritage Sites, London offers several other popular spots. Buckingham Palace is definitely one of them. It's the London residence and principal workplace of the monarchy of the United Kingdom. Located in the City of Westminster, the palace is often at the centre of state occasions and royal hospitality. It has been a focus for the British people at times of national rejoicing.

Originally known as Buckingham House, the building which forms the core of today's palace was a large townhouse built for the Duke of Buckingham in 1703 on a site which had been in private ownership for at least 150 years. It was subsequently acquired by King George III in 1761 as a private residence for Queen Charlotte and was known as "The Queen's House". During the 19th century it was enlarged, principally by architects John Nash and Edward Blore, who formed three wings around a central courtyard. Buckingham Palace finally became the official royal palace of the British monarch on the accession of Queen Victoria in 1837.

The last major structural additions were made in the late 19th and early 20th centuries, including the East front, which contains the well-known balcony on which the royal family traditionally congregates to greet crowds outside. However, the palace chapel was destroyed by a German bomb during World War II; the Queen's Gallery was built on the site and opened to the public in 1962 to exhibit works of art from the Royal Collection. Unlike the palace and the castle, the gallery is open continually and displays a changing selection of items from the collection on public display. The palace's state rooms have been open to the public during August and September since 1993. Book your tickets on their web site for a tour and timed entrance.

If you go by train, exit at London Victoria. The Tube serves 3 nearby stations: Victoria, Green Park and Hyde Park Corner. Bus numbers 11, 211, C1 and C10 stop on Buckingham Palace Road. The London Eye is a giant Ferris wheel on the South Bank of the River Thames in London. Also known as the Millennium Wheel. Since mid-January 2015, it has been known in branding as the Coca-Cola London Eye, following an agreement signed in September 2014.The entire structure is 135 meters tall and the wheel has a diameter of 120 meters. When erected in 1999 it was the world's tallest Ferris wheel. Its height was surpassed by the 160m Star of Nanchang in 2006, the 165m Singapore Flyer in 2008, and the 167.6m High Roller in Las Vegas in 2014. Supported by an A-frame on one side only, unlike the taller Nanchang and Singapore wheels, the Eye is described by its operators as "the world's tallest cantilevered observation wheel".It is currently Europe's tallest Ferris wheel. It offered the highest public viewing point in London until it was superseded by the 245 meter observation deck on the 72nd floor of The Shard, which opened to the public on February 1st 2013. It is the most popular paid tourist attraction in the United Kingdom with over 3.75 million visitors annually, and has made many appearances in popular culture.

The London Eye adjoins the western end of Jubilee Gardens, on the South Bank of the River Thames between Westminster Bridge and Hungerford Bridge, in the London Borough of Lambeth. The wheel's 32 sealed and air-conditioned ovoid passenger capsules are attached to the external circumference of the wheel and rotated by electric motors. Each of the capsules represents one of the London Boroughs and holds up to 25 people, who are free to walk around inside   the   capsule

, though seating is provided. One revolution takes about 30 minutes. It does not usually stop to take on passengers; the rotation rate is slow enough to allow passengers to walk on and off the moving capsules at ground level.

The nearest London Underground station is Waterloo, although Charing Cross, Embankment, and Westminster are also within easy walking distance. Connection with National Rail services is made at London Waterloo station and London Waterloo East station. London River Services operated by Thames Clippers and City Cruises stop at the London Eye Pier.

Another must see is the Piccadilly Circus. It is a road junction and public space of London's West End in the City of Westminster, built in 1819 to connect Regent Street with Piccadilly. In this context, a circus, from the Latin word meaning "circle", is a round open space at a street junction.

Piccadilly now links directly to the theatres on Shaftesbury Avenue, as well as the Haymarket, Coventry Street (onwards to Leicester Square), and Glasshouse Street. The Circus is close to major shopping and entertainment areas in the West End. Its status as a major traffic junction has made Piccadilly Circus a busy meeting place and a tourist attraction in its own right. The Circus is particularly known for its video display and neon signs mounted on the corner building on the northern side, as well as the Shaftesbury memorial fountain and statue of Eros. It is surrounded by several notable buildings, including the London Pavilion, Criterion Restaurant and Criterion Theatre. Directly underneath the plaza is Piccadilly Circus tube station, part of the London Underground system.

St Paul's Cathedral is an Anglican cathedral, the seat of the Bishop of London and the mother church of the Diocese of London. It sits at the top of Ludgate Hill, the highest point in the City of London. Its dedication to Paul the Apostle dates back to the original church on this site, founded in AD 604. The present church, dating from the late 17th century, was designed in the English Baroque style by Sir Christopher Wren. Its construction, completed within Wren's lifetime, was part of a major rebuilding program which took place in the city after the Great Fire of London.

The cathedral is one of the most famous and most recognizable sights of London, with its dome, framed by the spires of Wren's City churches, dominating the skyline for 300 years. At 111 meters high, it was the tallest building in London from 1710 to 1962, and its dome is also among the highest in the world. In terms of area, St Paul's is the second largest church building in the United Kingdom after Liverpool Cathedral.

St Paul's Cathedral occupies a significant place in the national identity of the English population. It is the central subject of much promotional material, as well as postcard images of the dome standing tall, surrounded by the smoke and fire of the Blitz. Important services held at St Paul's have included the funerals of Lord Nelson, the Duke of Wellington and Sir Winston Churchill; Jubilee celebrations for Queen Victoria; peace services marking the end of the First and Second World Wars; the wedding of Charles, Prince of Wales, and Lady Diana Spencer, the launch of the Festival of Britain and the thanksgiving services for the Golden Jubilee, the 80th Birthday and the Diamond Jubilee of Elizabeth II. St Paul's Cathedral is a busy working church, with hourly prayer and daily services.

The Interpretation Project is a long term project concerned with bringing St Paul's to life for all its visitors. In 2010, the Dean and Chapter of St Paul's opened St Paul's Oculus, a 270° film experience that brings 1400 years of history to life. Located in the former Treasury in the crypt, the film takes visitors on a journey through the history and daily life of St Paul's Cathedral. Oculus was funded by American Express Company in partnership with the World Monuments Fund, J. P. Morgan, the Garfield Weston Trust for St Paul's Cathedral, the City of London Endowment Trust and AIG.

In 2010, new touchscreen multimedia guides were also launched. These guides are included in the price of admission. Visitors can discover the cathedral's history, architecture and daily life of a busy working church with these new multimedia guides. They are available in 12 different languages. The guides have fly-through videos of the dome galleries and zoomable close-ups of the ceiling mosaics, painting and photography. Interviews and commentary from experts include the Dean of St Paul's, conservation team

Photo Credit 51:"An aerial view of St Paul'si" by Mark Fosh Licensed under CC BY 2.0 via Wikimedia Commons

and the Director of Music. Archive film footage includes major services and events from the cathedral's history.

St Paul's charges for the admission of those people who are sightseers, rather than worshippers; the charge is £18 (£15 when purchased online). Outside service times, people seeking a quiet place to pray or worship are admitted to St Dunstan's Chapel free of charge. On Sundays people are admitted only for services and there is no sightseeing. The cathedral explains that the charge to sightseers is because St Paul's receives little regular or significant funding from the Crown, Church or the State and relies on the income generated by tourism to allow the building to continue to function as a centre for Christian worship, as well as to cover general maintenance and repair work.

St. Paul's Tube Station is a 2 minute walk away from St Paul's. Mansion House Tube Station and Blackfriars Tube Station are around 5 minutes of walk away. DLR also serves St Paul's, stations are Bank and Tower Gateway.

Tower Bridge was built 1886–1894. It's a combined bascule and suspension bridge which crosses the River Thames. It is close to the Tower of London and has become an iconic symbol of London. The bridge's present color scheme dates from 1977, when it was painted red, white and blue for Queen Elizabeth II's Silver Jubilee. Originally it was painted a mid-greenish-blue.

The nearest London Underground tube stations are Tower Hill on the Circle and District lines, London Bridge and Bermondsey, and the nearest Docklands Light Railway station is Tower Gateway.

Trafalgar Square is a public space and tourist attraction in central London, built around the area formerly known as Charing Cross. It is situated in the City of Westminster. At its ce

Photo Credit 52:"Tower Bridge opening at night for a ferry" by Kashif H. Licensed under CC BY-SA 3.0 via Wikimedia Commons

ntre is Nelson's Column, which is guarded by four lion statues at its base. There are a number of commemorative statues and sculptures in the square, while one plinth, left empty since it was built in 1840, The Fourth Plinth, has been host to contemporary art since 1999. The square is also used for political demonstrations and community gatherings, such as the celebration of New Year's Eve.

The name commemorates the Battle of Trafalgar, a British naval victory of the Napoleonic Wars over France and Spain which took place in 1805 off the coast of Cape Trafalgar, Spain. The original name was to have been "King William the Fourth's Square", but George Ledwell Taylor suggested the name "Trafalgar Square".

In the 1820s George IV engaged the architect John Nash to redevelop the area. Nash cleared the square as part of his Charing Cross Improvement Scheme. The present architecture of the square is due to Sir Charles Barry and was completed in 1845.

Nearest London Underground stations are Charing Cross – Northern and Bakerloo Lines. They have an exit in the square. The two lines originally had separate stations, of which the Bakerloo line one was called Trafalgar Square; they were linked and renamed in 1979 as part of the construction of the Jubilee line, which was later rerouted to Westminster t

Photo Credit 53: "Trafalgar Square" by Diliff
Licensed under CC BY-SA 3.0 via Wikimedia Commons

ube station in late 1999. You can also exit at Embankment – District, Circle, Northern and Bakerloo lines; and Leicester Square – Northern and Piccadilly lines. Bus routes running through Trafalgar Square are 6, 9, 11, 12, 13, 15, 23, 24, 29, 53, 87, 88, 91, 139, 159, 176 and 453.

The Shard, also referred to as London Bridge Tower, is an 87-storey skyscraper in Southwark, London that forms part of the London Bridge Quarter development. The Shard's construction began in March 2009; it was inaugurated on 5 July 2012. Practical completion was achieved in November 2012. The tower's privately operated observation deck, the View from the Shard, was opened to the public on February 1st 2013.

Standing at 309.6 meters high, The Shard is currently the tallest building in the European Union. It is also the second-tallest free-standing structure in the United Kingdom, after the concrete tower at the Emley Moor transmitting station. The glass-clad pyramidal tower has 72 habitable floors, with a viewing gallery and open-air observation deck on the 72nd floor, at a height of 244.3 meters. It was designed by the Italian architect Renzo Piano and replaced Southwark Towers, a 24-storey office block built on the site in 1975.

Underground and mainline trains come into London Bridge station, which is directly next to The Shard and a short journey from other major transport hubs in London.

Chapter 5: Museums And Galleries

London hosts an outstanding collection of world-class museums, including three of the world's most visited. You can find nearly 250 other museums across the city. Best of all, many of these let you see their permanent collections for free, including must-visit places. In contrast to this, independent museums will usually charge you to enter. This is also true of temporary exhibitions at the free-to-enter museums. Although amounts differ, it is usually around £10-£15. However, the money-conscious tourist can see a significant number of masterpieces without having to spend a penny.

London also has over 250 art galleries. Although some require an appointment and/or have limited opening hours, most are open to the public and free to visit. From the classical to the contemporary, all forms of art imaginable can be seen in London. Work from famous artists, from Da Vinci to Damien Hirst can be seen in the city, alongside thousands of other world-famous works and the famous works of the future. The British Museum is a museum dedicated to human history, art, and culture, located in the Bloomsbury area of London. Its permanent collection, numbering some 8 million works, is among the largest and most comprehensive in existence and originates from all continents, illustrating and documenting the story of human culture from its beginnings to the present. This is London's most popular museum and the second most-visited in the world.

Photo Credit 55:"Façade of the British Museum" by Ham
Licensed under CC BY-SA 3.0 via Wikimedia Commons

The British Museum was established in 1753, largely based on the collections of the physician and scientist Sir Hans Sloane. The museum first opened to the public on January 15th 1759 in Montagu House in Bloomsbury, on the site of the current museum building. Its expansion over the following two and a half centuries was largely a result of an expanding British colonial footprint and has resulted in the creation of several branch institutions, the first being the British Museum (Natural History) in South Kensington in 1881. Some objects in the collection, most notably the Elgin Marbles from the Parthenon, are the objects of controversy and of calls for restitution to their countries of origin.

The museum is a non-departmental public body sponsored by the Department for Culture, Media and Sport, and as with all other national museums in the United Kingdom it charges no admission fee, except for loan exhibitions.

The British Museum houses the world's largest and most comprehensive collection of Egyptian antiquities outside the Egyptian Museum in Cairo. A collection of immense importance for its range and quality, it includes objects of all periods from virtually every site of importance in Egypt and the Sudan.

It also has one of the world's largest and most comprehensive collections of antiquities from the Classical world, with over 100,000 objects. These mostly range in date from the beginning of the Greek Bronze Age (about 3200 BC) to the establishment of Christianity as the official religion of the Roman Empire, with the Edict of Milan under the reign of the Roman Emperor Constantine in 313 AD.

The British Museum possesses the world's largest and most important collection of Mesopotamian antiquities outside Iraq. The collections represent the civilizations of the ancient Near East and its adjacent areas. Only the Middle East collections of the Louvre and the Pergamon Museum rival it in the range and quality of artifacts.

The Department of Prints and Drawings holds the national collection of Western prints and drawings. It ranks as one of the largest and best print room collections in existence alongside the Albertina in Vienna and the Paris collections and the Hermitage. The holdings are easily accessible to the general public in the Study Room.

The Department of Prehistory and Europe was established in 1969 and is responsible for collections that cover a vast expanse of time and geography. It includes some of the earliest objects made by humans in east Africa over 2 million years ago, as well as Prehistoric and Neolithic objects from other parts of the world.

Photo Credit 56:"British museum entrance" by Jon Sullivan
Licensed under Public Domain via Wikimedia Commons

In addition, the British Museum's collections covering the period AD 300 to 1100 are among the largest and most comprehensive in the world, extending from Spain to the Black Sea and from North Africa to Scandinavia; a representative selection of these has recently been redisplayed in a newly refurbished gallery.

The scope of the Department of Asia is extremely broad; its collections of over 75,000 objects cover the material culture of the whole Asian continent and from the Neolithic up to the present day. Until recently, this department concentrated on collecting Oriental antiquities from urban or semi-urban societies across the Asian continent. Many of those objects were collected by colonial officers and explorers in former parts of the British Empire, especially the Indian subcontinent.

Key highlights of the collections include: the most comprehensive collection of sculpture from the Indian subcontinent in the world, including the celebrated Buddhist limestone reliefs from Amaravati excavated by Sir Walter Elliot; an outstanding collection of Chinese antiquities, paintings, and porcelain, lacquer, bronze, jade, and other applied arts; the most comprehensive collection of Japanese pre-20th century art in the Western world, many of which originally belonged to the surgeon William Anderson and diplomat Ernest Mason Satow.

The British Museum houses one of the world's most comprehensive collections of Ethnographic material from Africa, Oceania and the Americas, representing the cultures of indigenous peoples throughout the world. Over 350,000 objects spanning thousands of years tells the history of mankind from three major continents and many rich and diverse cultures.

The British Museum is also home to one of the world's finest numismatic collections, comprising about a million objects, including coins, medals, tokens and paper money. The collection spans the entire history of coinage from its origins in the 7th century BC to the present day and is representative of both the East and West. As in other parts of the museum, the department has been able to expand its collection by purchase, donation and bequest. Items from the full collection can be seen by the general public in the Study Room by appointment.

The department of Conservation and Scientific was founded in 1920. Conservation has six specialist areas: ceramics & glass; metals; organic material (including textiles); stone, wall paintings and mosaics; Eastern pictorial art and Western pictorial art. The science department has and continues to develop techniques to date artifacts, analyze and identify the materials used in their manufacture, to identify the place an artifact originated and the techniques used in their creation. The department also publishes its findings and discoveries.

The Libraries and Archives department covers all levels of education, from casual visitors, schools, degree level and beyond. The Museum's various libraries hold in excess of 350,000 books, journals and pamphlets covering all areas of the museum's collection. Also the general Museum archives which date from its foundation in 1753 are overseen by this department

Nearest underground stations are Holborn (500m), Tottenham Court Road (500m), Russell Square (800m) and Goodge Street (800m). Buses that stop near the Museum: 1, 7, 8, 19, 25, 38, 55, 98, 242 on New Oxford Street. Numbers 10, 14, 24, 29, 73, 134, 390 stop northbound on Tottenham Court Road and southbound on Gower Street; and 59, 68, X68, 91, 168, 188 stop on Southampton Row. The National Gallery is an art museum in Trafalgar Square located in the City of Westminster, in Central London. Founded in 1824, it houses a collection of over 2,300 paintings dating from the mid-13th century to 1900. Its collection belongs to the public of the United Kingdom and entry to the main collection is free of charge. It is among the most visited art museums in the world, after the Musée du Louvre, the British Museum, and the Metropolitan Museum of Art.

Unlike comparable museums in continental Europe, the National Gallery was not formed by nationalizing an existing royal or princely art collection. It came into being when the British government bought

38 paintings from the heirs of John Julius Angerstein, an insurance broker and patron of the arts, in 1824.

The gallery houses a collection is small in size, compared with many European national galleries, but encyclopedic in scope; most major developments in Western painting "from Giotto to Cézanne" are represented with important works. It used to be claimed that this was one of the few national galleries that had all its works on permanent exhibition, but this is no longer the case.

To get there, exit the Tube at Westminster station. This is the nearest station with a lift.

Embankment tube station, Piccadilly tube station, Leicester Square tube station and Charing Cross tube and railway station are also close to the museum.

The Victoria and Albert Museum (often abbreviated as the V&A) is the world's largest museum of decorative arts and design, housing a permanent collection of over 4.5 million objects. It was founded in 1852 and named after Queen Victoria and Prince Albert. The V&A is located in the Brompton district of the Royal Borough of Kensington and Chelsea, in an area that has become known as "Albertopolis". Like other national British museums, entrance to the museum has been free since 2001.

The V&A covers 51,000 m2 and 145 galleries. Its collection spans 5,000 years of art, from ancient times to the present day, from the cultures of Europe, North America, Asia and North Africa. The holdings of ceramics, glass, textiles, costumes, silver, ironwork, jewelry, furniture, medieval objects, sculpture, prints and printmaking, drawings and photographs are among the largest and most comprehensive in the world. The museum owns the world's largest collection of post-classical sculpture, with the holdings of

Italian Renaissance items being the largest outside Italy. The departments of Asia include art from South Asia, China, Japan, Korea and the Islamic world. The East Asian collections are among the best in Europe, with particular strengths in ceramics and metalwork, while the Islamic collection is amongst the largest in the Western world.

Since 2001, the museum has embarked on a major £150m renovation program which has seen a major overhaul of the departments, including the introduction of newer galleries, gardens, shops and visitor facilities.

The Victoria & Albert Museum is split into four collections departments. The collection departments are further divided into sixteen display areas, whose combined collection numbers over 6.5 million objects, not all items are displayed or stored at the V&A.

The Museum is less than five minute walk from Bethnal Green Underground station. Buses D6, 106, 254, 309 and 388 stop outside the Museum and 8, 26, 55 and 48 stop nearby. The Museum is less than 10 minute walk from both Cambridge Heath and Bethnal Green railway stations. The nearest main line station is Liverpool Street, which is less than a five minute Underground journey from Bethnal Green.

The Natural History Museum in London is a museum exhibiting a vast range of specimens from various segments of natural history. It is one of three major museums on Exhibition Road in South Kensington, the others being the Science Museum and the Victoria and Albert Museum. The Natural History Museum's main frontage, however, is on Cromwell Road.

The museum is home to life and earth science specimens comprising some 80 million items within five main collections: botany, entomology, mineralogy, paleontology and zoology. The museum is a world-renowned centre of research specializing in taxonomy, identification and conservation. Given the age of the institution, many of the collections have great historical as well as scientific value, such as specimens collected by Charles Darwin. The museum is particularly famous for its exhibition of dinosaur skeletons and ornate architecture—sometimes dubbed a cathedral of nature—both exemplified by

the large Diplodocus cast which dominates the vaulted central hall. The Natural History Museum Library contains extensive books, journals, manuscripts, and artwork collections linked to the work and research of the scientific departments; access to the library is by appointment only.

Like other publicly funded national museums in the United Kingdom, the Natural History Museum does not charge an admission fee.

The nearest Tube station is South Kensington on the District, Piccadilly and Circle lines. The station is approximately five minutes' walk from the Museum. Also, bus routes 14, 49, 70, 74, 345, 360, 414, 430 and C1 stop close to the Museum.

The Science Museum is another major museum on Exhibition Road in South Kensington. It was founded in 1857 and today is one of the city's major tourist attractions, attracting 3.3 million visitors annually.

When Queen Victoria laid the foundation stone for the new building for the Art Museum, she stipulated that the museum be renamed after herself and her late husband. This was initially applied to the whole museum, but when that new building finally opened ten years later, the title was confined to the Art Collections and the Science Collections had to be divorced from it. On June 26th 1909 the Science Museum, as an independent entity, came into existence.

The Science Museum's present quarters, designed by Sir Richard Allison, were opened to the public in stages over the period 1919–28.

The Science Museum now holds a collection of over 300,000 items, including such famous items as Stephenson's Rocket, Puffing Billy (the oldest surviving steam locomotive), the first jet engine, a reconstruction of Francis Crick and James Watson's model of DNA, some of the earliest remaining steam engines, a working example of Charles Babbage's Difference engine, the first prototype of the 10,000-year Clock of the Long Now, and documentation of the first typewriter. It also contains hundreds of interactive exhibits. A recent addition is the IMAX 3D Cinema showing science and nature documentaries, most of them in 3D, and the Welcome Wing which focuses on digital technology.

The nearest tube station is South Kensington. A pedestrian subway connects South Kensington station to the main entrance. Gloucester Road tube station is also close, only a 15 minute walk away. Bus routes 14, 49, 70, 74, 345, 360, 414, 430 and C1 stop outside South Kensington Underground Station, while bus routes 9, 10, 52, 452 and 70 stop outside the Royal Albert Hall on Kensington Gore. The National Portrait Gallery (NPG) is an art gallery in London housing a collection of portraits of historically important and famous British people. It was the first portrait gallery in the world when it opened in 1856. The gallery moved in 1896 to its current site at St Martin's

Place, off Trafalgar Square. It has been expanded twice since then.

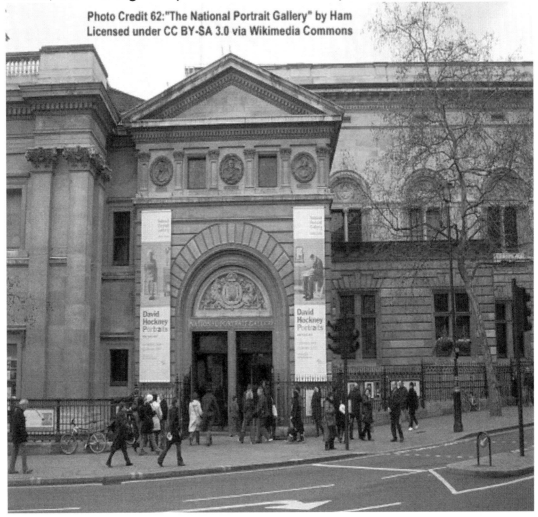

The gallery houses portraits of historically important and famous British people, selected on the basis of the significance of the sitter, not that of the artist. The collection includes photographs and caricatures as well as paintings, drawings and sculpture. One of its best-known images is the Chandos portrait, the most famous portrait of William Shakespeare, although there is some uncertainty about whether the painting actually is of the playwright.

Portraits of living figures were allowed from 1969. In addition to its permanent galleries of historical portraits, the National Portrait Gallery exhibits a rapidly changing selection of contemporary work, stages exhibitions of portrait art by individual artists and hosts the annual BP Portrait Prize competition.

The nearest underground stations to the Gallery are: Charing Cross, Leicester Square and Embankment. By train Charing Cross station is the closest one to the St Martin's Place entrance. Bus numbers 24, 29 and 176 from Trafalgar Square. exit at stop C or Charing Cross Road stop K.

Tate Britain is an art gallery situated on Millbank in London. It is part of the Tate network of galleries in England, with Tate Modern, Tate Liverpool and Tate St Ives. It is the oldest gallery in the network, having opened in 1897. It houses a substantial collection of the works of J. M. W. Turner.

Construction commenced in 1893 and the gallery opened on in July 1897 as the National Gallery of British Art. However, from the start it was commonly known as the Tate Gallery, after its founder Sir Henry Tate. In 1932 it officially adopted that name. Before 2000, the gallery housed and displayed both British and modern collections, but the launch of Tate Modern saw Tate's modern collections move there, while the old Millbank gallery became dedicated to the display of historical and contemporary British art. As a consequence, it was renamed Tate Britain in March 2000.

The main display spaces show the permanent collection of historic British art, as well as contemporary work. The gallery also organizes career retrospectives of British artists and temporary major exhibitions of British Art. Every three years the gallery stages a Triennial exhibition in which a guest curator provides an overview of contemporary British Art.

Regular free tours operate on the hour, and at 1.15pm on Tuesday, Wednesday and Thursday short 15 minute talks are given on paintings, artists and artistic styles.

The nearest London Underground stations to Tate Britain are: Pimlico, Vauxhall and Westminster. The following buses stop near Tate Britain: route 87 stops on Millbank, routes 88 and C10 stop on John Islip Street and routes 2, 36, 185, 436 stop on Vauxhall Bridge Road. The nearest mainline train stations to Tate Britain are: Vauxhall and Victoria.

Tate Modern is a modern art gallery located in London. It is Britain's national gallery of international modern art and forms part of the Tate group. It is based in the former Bankside Power Station, in the Bankside area of the London Borough of Southwark. Tate holds the national collection of British art from 1900 to the present day and international modern and contemporary art.

The galleries are housed in the former Bankside Power Station, which was originally designed by Sir Giles Gilbert Scott, and built in two stages between 1947 and 1963. The power station closed in 1981. In 1992 The Tate Gallery at the British National Art Museum proposed a competition to build a new building for modern art. The purpose for the new building would help with the ever-expanding collection on modern and contemporary art. In 1995 it was announced that Herzog & de Meuron had won the competition with their simple design. The architects decided to reinvent the current building instead of demolishing it. The Tate modern is an example of adaptive reuse, the process of finding new life in old buildings. The building itself still resembles the 20th century factory in style from the outside and that is reflected on the inside by the taupe walls, steel girders and concrete floors. The façade of the building is made out of 4.2 million bricks that are separated by groups of thin vertical windows that help create a dramatic light inside. The history of the site as well as information about the conversion was the basis for a 2008 documentary Architects Herzog and de Meuron: Alchemy of Building & Tate Modern.

The nearest London Underground stations to Tate Modern are: Southwark, Blackfriars and St Paul's. The following buses stop near Tate Modern: routes 45, 63 and 100 stop on Blackfriars Bridge Road, routes RV1 and 381 stop on Southwark Street and route 344 stops on Southwark Bridge Road. The nearest mainline train stations to Tate Modern are: Blackfriars and London Bridge.

Chapter 6: The 'Green Lungs' Of London

The Royal Parks of London are lands originally owned by the monarchy of the United Kingdom for the recreation of the royal family. They are part of the hereditary possessions of The Crown. With increasing urbanization of London, some of these were preserved as freely accessible open space and became public parks with the introduction of the Crown Lands Act 1851. There are today eight parks formally described by this name and they cover almost 2,000 hectares (of land in Greater London.

The largest parks in the central area of London are three of the eight Royal Parks, namely Hyde Park and its neighbor Kensington Gardens in the west, and Regent's Park to the north.

Hyde Park is one of the largest parks in London, famous for its Speakers' Corner. The park was the site of the Great Exhibition of 1851, for which the Crystal Palace was designed by Joseph Paxton.

The park is divided in two by the Serpentine and the Long Water. It's contiguous with Kensington Gardens. Although often still assumed to be part of Hyde Park, Kensington Gardens has been technically separate since 1728, when Queen Caroline made a division between the two. Hyde Park covers 142 hectares and Kensington Gardens covers 111 hectares giving an overall area of 253 hectares. To the southeast, outside the park, is Hyde Park Corner. Although, during daylight, the two parks merge seamlessly into each other, Kensington Gardens closes at dusk but Hyde Park remains open throughout the year from 5 am until midnight.

Sites of interest in the park include Speakers' Corner (located in the northeast corner near Marble Arch), close to the former site of the Tyburn gallows, and Rotten Row, which is the northern boundary of the site of the Crystal Palace. South of the Serpentine is the Diana, Princess of Wales memorial, an oval stone ring fountain opened in 2004. To the east of the Serpentine, just beyond the dam, is London's Holocaust Memorial. The 7 July Memorial in the park commemorates the victims of July 7th 2005 London bombings.

Photo Credit 66: "The 7 July Memorial" by Nick Cooper
Licensed under CC BY 3.0 via Wikimedia Commons

A botanical curiosity is the Weeping Beech, cherished as "the upside-down tree". Opposite Hyde Park Corner stands one of the grandest hotels in London, The Lanesborough. A rose garden, designed by Colvin & Moggridge Landscape Architects, was added in 1994.

An assortment of unusual sculptures are scattered around the park, including Drinking Horse, made in the shape of a massive horse head lapping up water, a family of Jelly Babies standing on top of a large black cube, and Vroom Vroom, which resembles a giant human hand pushing a toy car along the ground.

There are five London Underground stations located on or near the edges of Hyde Park and Kensington Gardens. In clockwise order starting from the south-east, they are: Hyde Park Corner (Piccadilly line), Knightsbridge (Piccadilly line), Queensway (Central line), Lancaster Gate (Central line) and Marble Arch (Central line).

Kensington Gardens, once the private gardens of Kensington Palace are located immediately to the west of Hyde Park. It is shared between the City of Westminster and the Royal Borough of Kensington and Chelsea, lying within western central London. The open spaces of Kensington Gardens, Hyde Park, Green Park and St. James's Park together form an almost continuous "green lung" in the heart of London between Kensington and Westminster.

Kensington Gardens are generally regarded as being the western extent of the neighboring Hyde Park from which they were originally taken, with West Carriage Drive (The Ring) and the Serpentine Bridge forming the boundary between them. The Gardens are fenced and more formal than Hyde Park. Kensington Gardens are open only during the hours of daylight.

The land surrounding Kensington Gardens was predominantly rural and remained largely undeveloped until the Great Exhibition in 1851. Many of the original features survive along with the Palace, and now there are other public buildings such as the Albert Memorial, the Serpentine Gallery, and Speke's monument. The park also contains the Elfin Oak, an elaborately carved 900-year-old tree stump.

Kensington Gardens is readily accessible by public transport. There are a number of tube stations and bus stops that surround the park. The tube stations that surround Kensington Gardens are: Lancaster Gate & Queensway (Central Line), Bayswater (District Line) and High Street Kensington (Circle and District Lines).

Green Park is located in the City of Westminster, central London. One of the Royal Parks of London, it covers 19 hectares between Hyde Park and St. James's Park. Together with Kensington Gardens and the gardens of Buckingham Palace, these parks form an almost unbroken stretch of open land reaching from Whitehall and Victoria station to Kensington and Notting Hill.

By contrast with its neighboring parks, Green Park has no lakes, no buildings and few monuments, having only the Canada Memorial by Pierre Granche, the Diana Fountain and the RAF Bomber Command Memorial. Instead the park consists almost entirely of mature trees rising out of turf; the only flowers are naturalized narcissus.

The park is bounded on the south by Constitution Hill, on the east by the pedestrian Queen's Walk, and on the north by Piccadilly. It meets St. James's Park at Queen's Gardens with the Victoria Memorial at its centre, opposite the entrance to Buckingham Palace.

To the south is the ceremonial avenue of the Mall, and the buildings of St James's Palace and Clarence House overlook the park to the east.

Green Park tube station is a major interchange located on Piccadilly, Victoria and Jubilee lines near the north end of Queen's Walk. Tyburn stream runs beneath Green Park.

St. James's Park is a 23 hectares park in the City of Westminster in central London. The park lies at the southernmost tip of the St James' area, which was named after a leper hospital dedicated to St. James the Less. The park is the most easterly of a near-continuous chain of parks that also comprises (moving

westward) Green Park, Hyde Park, and Kensington Gardens. St. James' Park is bounded by Buckingham Palace to the west, The Mall to the north, Horse Guards to the east, and Birdcage Walk to the south. It meets Green Park at Queen's Gardens with the Victoria Memorial at its centre, opposite the entrance to Buckingham Palace. St. James's Palace lie

s on the opposite side of The Mall.

The park has a small lake, St. James's Park Lake, with two islands, West Island, and Duck Island, which is named for the lake's collection of waterfowl. This includes a resident colony of pelicans, which has been a feature of the park since the first gift of the birds from a Russian ambassador in 1664. The Blue Bridge across the lake affords a view west towards Buckingham Palace framed by trees. Looking east the view includes the Swire fountain to the north of Duck Island and, past the lake, the grounds known as the Horse Guards Parade, with the Horse Guards building, the Old War Office building, and Whitehall Court progressively behind. To the south of Duck Island is the Tiffany fountain situated on Pelican Rock, and past the lake is the Foreign and Commonwealth Office, with the London Eye, the Shell Tower, and The Shard progressively behind.

The closest London Underground stations are St. James's Park, Green Park, Victoria, and Westminster.

The Regent's Park is one of the Royal Parks of London. It lies within north-west London, partly in the City of Westminster and partly in the London Borough of Camden. It contains Regent's University London and the London Zoo.

The park has an outer ring road called the Outer Circle (4.45 km) and an inner ring road called the Inner Circle (1 km), which surrounds the most carefully tended section of the park, Queen Mary's Gardens. Apart from two link roads

between these two, the park is reserved for pedestrians. The south, east and most of the west side of the park are lined with elegant white stucco terraces of houses designed by John Nash. Running through the northern end of the park is Regent's Canal, which connects the Grand Union Canal to the former London docks.

The 166 hectares park is mainly open parkland that enjoys a wide range of facilities and amenities including gardens, a lake with a heronry, waterfowl and a boating area, sports pitches, and children's playgrounds. The northern side of the park is the home of London Zoo and the headquarters of the Zoological Society of London. There are several public gardens with flowers and specimen plants, including Queen Mary's Gardens in the Inner Circle, in which the Open Air Theatre is located; the formal Italian Gardens and adjacent informal English Gardens in the south-east corner of the park; and the gardens of St John's Lodge. Winfield House, the official residence of the U.S. Ambassador to the United Kingdom, stands in private grounds in the western section of the park. Nearby is the domed London Central Mosque, better known as Regent's Park mosque, a highly visible landmark.

Located to the south of the Inner Circle is Regent's University London, home of the European Business School London, Regent's American College London (RACL) and Webster Graduate School among others.

On the northern side of Regent's Park is Primrose Hill, which with a height of 78m gives has a clear view of central London to the south-east, as well as Belsize Park and Hampstead to the north. Primrose Hill is also the name given to the surrounding district.

Nearest Tube stations are: Regent's Park, Baker Street and Great Portland Street. Nearest railway stations are Camden Road and Marylebone.

A number of large parks lie outside the city centre, including the remaining Royal Parks of Greenwich Park to the south-east and Bushy Park and Richmond Park to the south-west. Hampton Court Park is also a royal park, but, because it contains a palace, it is administered by the Historic Royal Palaces, unlike the eight Royal Parks.

Greenwich Park is a former hunting park in Greenwich and one of the largest single green spaces in south-east London. This is the first park to be enclosed in 1433. It covers 74 hectares and is part of the Greenwich World Heritage Site. It commands fine views over the River Thames, the Isle of Dogs and the City of London. The park is open from 06:00 for pedestrians (and 07:00 for traffic) all year round and closes at dusk.

The park stretches along a hillside and is on two levels. The lower level (closest to the Museum, Queen's House and, beyond them, the Thames) lies to the north; after a steep walk uphill, there is a flat expanse that is, essentially, an enclosed extension of the plateau of Blackheath.

Roughly in the centre, on the top of the hill, is the Royal Observatory. To the north is the National Maritime Museum and Queen's House, and beyond those Greenwich Hospital. To the east is Vanbrugh Castle. To the south is Blackheath and in the south western corner is the Ranger's House, looking out over heath. To the west lie the architecturally fine streets of Chesterfield Walk and Croom's Hill.

On the lower level of the park there is a popular children's playground (north-east corner, close to Maze Hill railway station) and an adjacent boating lake. There is also a herb garden (close by entrance to Greenwich town centre).

On the upper level, there is an extensive flower garden complete with large duck pond, a rose garden, a cricket pitch, many 17th century chestnut trees with gnarled, swirling trunks, tennis courts, a bandstand, Roman remains, an ancient oak tree (the 'Queens Oak', associated with Queen Elizabeth I) and an enclosure ('The Wilderness') housing some wild deer.

Nestling just behind the Observatory is the garden of the former Astronomer Royal, a peaceful secluded space which is good for picnics and also sometimes used by theatre groups (Midsummer Night's Dream, etc.). On the opposite side (i.e., just south of the Wolfe statue) is the Park Café. There is another, smaller café by the north-west gate.

Greenwich Park is well-served by bus routes and is within walking distance of Blackheath, Greenwich and Maze Hill railway stations. Exit at North Greenwich (Jubilee Line) - then catch the 188 bus to Greenwich Park gate. Connecting trains depart from Cannon Street, Waterloo, London Bridge and Charing Cross and go to Greenwich, Maze Hill and Blackheath. If you take Dockland Light Railway exit at Cutty Sark station then walk through the market and you will reach St Mary's Gate and the Circus Gates of the park. You can also exit at Greenwich station and follow the signs to the park. Bus routes to the park are: 53, 54, 177, 180, 188, 199, 202, 286, 380 and 386.

Bushy Park is located in the London Borough of Richmond upon Thames and it's the second largest of London's Royal Parks with 445 hectares in area. The park, most of which is open to the public, is immediately north of Hampton Court Palace and Hampton Court Park and is a few minutes' walk from the north side of Kingston Bridge. It is surrounded by Teddington, Hampton, Hampton Hill and Hampton Wick, and lies within the post towns of East Molesey, Hampton, Kingston upon Thames and Teddington.

Photo Credit 72:"Chestnut trees in early autumn, Bushy Park" by Ojw
Licensed under CC BY-SA 3.0 via Wikimedia Commons

The park's acid grasslands are mostly just above the 25-foot contour. In September 2014 most of it was designated a biological Site of Special Scientific Interest together with Hampton Court Park and Hampton Court Golf Course as Bushy Park and Home Park SSSI.

Originally created for royal sports, Bushy Park is now home to Teddington Rugby Club, Teddington Hockey Club and four cricket clubs. It also has fishing and model boating ponds, horse rides, formal plantations of trees and other plants, wildlife conservation areas and herds of both red deer and fallow deer.

The park also contains several lodges and cottages, Bushy House, the National Physical Laboratory (NPL) at the Teddington end, the Royal Paddocks, and two areas of allotments: the Royal Paddocks Allotments at Hampton Wick and the Bushy Park Allotments at Hampton Hill.

As part of an upgrade of the park facilities, the new Pheasantry Café was added, and the restored and largely reconstructed Upper Lodge Water Gardens were opened in October 2009.

The closest railway stations are Hampton Court in East Molesey to the south, Hampton Wick to the east, Teddington and Fulwell to the north, and Hampton to the west. All are within a 10- to 20-minute walk. Transport for London bus routes 111, 216 and 411 pass the Hampton Court Gate on Hampton Court Road (the main southern entrance to the Park). R70, R68 and 285 buses stop near the two Hampton Hill Gates off the High Street, while the R68 also serves the Blandford Road Gate before continuing to Hampton Court Green via Hampton Hill. To the north the main Teddington gate on Park Road and a second on Sandy Lane are only served by an hourly 481 bus service. But the main gate is best reached, either on foot or by bike, from Teddington's town centre, via Park Road, or from the railway station.

Richmond Park in south-west London was created by Charles I in the 17th century as a deer park. The largest of London's Royal Parks, it is of national and international importance for wildlife conservation. The park is a national nature reserve, a Site of Special Scientific Interest and a Special Area of Conservation and is included, at Grade I, on Historic England's Register of Historic Parks and Gardens of special historic interest in England. Its landscapes have inspired many famous artists and it has been a location for several films and TV series.

Richmond Park includes many buildings of architectural or historic interest. The Grade I-listed White Lodge was formerly a royal residence and is now home to the Royal Ballet School. The park's boundary walls and ten other buildings are listed at Grade II, including Pembroke Lodge, the home of 19th-century British Prime Minister Lord John Russell and his grandson, the philosopher Bertrand Russell.

Historically the preserve of the monarch, the park is now open for all to use and includes a golf course and other facilities for sport and recreation. It played an important role in both world wars and in the 1948 and 2012 Olympics. From Easter until the end of August 2015, a free bus service runs on Wednesdays, stopping at the main car parks and the gate at Isabella Plantation nearest Peg's Pond. If you chose to visit the park using the Tube or train exit at Richmond Station - National Rail or District Line and then catch the 371 or 65 buses to the pedestrian gate at Petersham. Bus services also run to the park. Bus routes are 190, 391, 419 and R68. To the north side bus routes are 33, 337 and 485. To the south catch the 85/N85, 265 or K3. To arrive at the east side catch 72 or 493. And to the west, catch 65 or 371.

Photo Credit 73:"Park at Richmond Castle, Brunswick" by Heinz Kudalla
Licensed under Attribution via Wikimedia Commons

Close to Richmond Park is Kew Gardens which has the world's largest collection of living plants. There are also numerous parks administered by London's borough Councils, including Victoria Park in the East End and Battersea Park in the centre. Some more informal, semi-natural open spaces also exist, including the 320-hectare Hampstead Heath of North London and Epping Forest, which covers 2,476 hectares in the east. Hampstead Heath incorporates Kenwood House, the former stately home and a popular location in the summer months where classical musical concerts are held by the lake, attracting thousands of people every weekend to enjoy the music, scenery and fireworks. Epping Forest is a popular venue for various outdoor activities, including mountain biking, walking, horse riding, golf, angling, and orienteering.

Chapter 7: Best Shopping Districts And Streets

London is said to be home to around 40,000 shops selling everything under the sun. It has several distinct retail districts and shopping streets, many of which have their own themes or specialties. From luxury goods in Mayfair to quirky finds in Covent Garden, to large shopping centers like Westfield, you can easily while away an hour, an afternoon or a whole day shopping in London.

The heart of London shopping, bustling Oxford Street has more than 300 shops, designer outlets and landmark stores. Home to the legendary Selfridges, it also boasts a range of famous department stores such as John Lewis and Debenhams scattered among every well-known high street chain imaginable. Get off the beaten track by slipping into a side street, such as St Christopher's Place and Berwick Street, where you'll find some real

Photo Credit 74:"Oxford Street " by Ysangkok
Licensed under Public Domain via Wikimedia Commons

treats.

Nearest tube to Oxford Street is Oxford Circus, Bond Street or Tottenham Court Road.

An impressively elegant shopping street, Regent Street offers a good range of mid-priced fashion stores alongside some of the city's oldest and most famous shops, including Hamleys, Liberty and The Apple Store. Nearby, historic Jermyn Street is renowned for men's clothing shops and is so typically British it's enough to bring out the old-fashioned gent in anyone! Jermyn Street is particularly well known for its bespoke shirt makers such as Benson & Clegg and shoe shops including John Lobb. Nearest Tube is the Piccadilly Circus or Oxford Circus.

Whether you've got money to burn and want to splash out on the very best in designer clothes, or just love luxury window shopping, Bond Street and Mayfair are the ideal places to go for some extravagant retail therapy. Popular with celebrities on a spree, this is probably London's most exclusive shopping area, home to big names, including Burberry, Louis Vuitton and Tiffany & Co. Neighboring South Molton Street boasts iconic fashion store, Browns. Nearest Tube is Bond Street or Piccadilly Circus.

Westfield has two major shopping malls in London at White City and Stratford. Westfield London is home to high street favorites including Debenhams, Next, Marks & Spencer and House of Fraser, along with luxury brands, such as Louis Vuitton, Jimmy Choo, All Saints and Ted Baker. There's also a cinema, gym, several bars and restaurants, all under one roof! If you're a fan of shopping centers, don't miss Westfield Stratford City in East London, which boasts 250 shops plus 70 places to dine, making it the largest shopping mall in Europe.

Nearest tube are White City or Shepherds Bush for Westfield London, and Stratford for Westfield Stratford City.

The birthplace of the fashion and cultural revolution during the Swinging 60s, Carnaby Street and the 13 surrounding streets are two minutes away from Oxford Circus and Piccadilly Circus and feature more than 150 brands and over 50 independent restaurants and bars. Step under the iconic arch and you'll find an intriguing mix of stores as well as independent boutiques, heritage brands, and new designer names, as well as a choice of restaurants, bars, cafés and great English pubs will real ale, and real history. Refuel at restaurant hub Kingly Court, just off Carnaby Street. The nearest

Tube is Oxford Circus or Piccadilly Circus.

Whether you want hip fashion, unique gifts, rare sweets or one-off handmade jewelry, Covent Garden is a great place to explore. You can stock up on the latest urban streetwear, funky cosmetics and shoes on Neal Street, check out imaginative arts and crafts at Covent Garden Market or just window shop around the stores. Don't miss Floral

Photo Credit 77:"Covent Garden Interior" by SilkTork Licensed under CC BY 2.5 via Wikimedia Commons

Street, Monmouth Street, St Martin's Courtyard, Shorts Gardens, Seven Dials and picture-pretty Neal's Yard for a true taste of

London's most distinctive shopping area. The nearest Tube is Covent Garden or Leicester Square.

Shopping is the King's Road's main obsession – here you'll find an eclectic mix of trendy boutiques, unique labels, designer shops and high-street staples, alongside a vast array of cafes and eateries. It's also a great place for inspirational interior design, with Peter Jones, Heal's and Cath Kidston all vying for attention. Be sure to check out the store where punk was born in the 70s, Vivienne Westwood's shop and the treasure trove of antiques at the Chelsea Antiques Market. The nearest Tube is Sloane Square.

Visitors from around the world flock to Knightsbridge and Brompton Road to visit the illustrious shops and department stores. This is the place to go if you're looking for prestigious brands and up-to-the-minute trends from the world's fashion elite. Best known for Harrods and Harvey Nichols, you'll also find a whole host of big-name fashion designers on Sloane Street. Showing Knightsbridge caters to all tastes, there's a branch of Topshop opposite Harrods. The nearest Tube station is Knightsbridge.

Known worldwide as the home of bespoke British tailoring, Savile Row is the place to come if you want a handmade suit crafted the old-fashioned way (with a price tag to match). Credited with inventing the tuxedo Henry Poole & Co – also the first Savile Row tailor – is still cutting cloth at No 15. Other big names include Gieves & Hawkes, Huntsman & Sons and Ozwald Boateng. On the corner of this "golden mile" of tailoring you'll also find the flagship Abercrombie & Fitch store. The nearest Tube stations are Bond Street or Piccadilly Circus. Famous worldwide thanks to the film of the same name, Notting Hill offers a vast array of small, unique shops selling unusual and vintage clothing, rare antiques, quirky gifts, books and organic food. There's also the unmissable Portobello Road Market – a mile-long (1.6km) street with a vibrant array of different stalls set out daily. Nearby Westbourne Grove offers more high-end shopping, with stylish designer shops dotted between a mix of quirky boho boutiques, hip cafes and art galleries. Nearest Tube stations are Notting Hill Gate, Ladbroke Grove or

Westbourne Park. Canada Square, in London's Docklands, is home to many of the UK's leading businesses, but it also has a great shopping centre, open seven days a week. Sleek and modern, Canada Square boasts more than 200 shops, with all the major high-street chains as well as a good selection of designer stores. Look out for big names like Oasis and Zara plus lingerie brand Myla and luxurious fragrance store Jo Malone. If you can avoid the weekday lunch-hour rush, it's one of London's

Photo Credit 80: "Notting Hill" by Urban
Licensed under CC BY-SA 2.5 via Wikimedia Commons

most chilled-out shopping experiences. The nearest Tube station is

Canary Wharf.

Based in the heart of East London, Boxpark Shoreditch is the world's first pop-up mall and the home of the pop-up store. Opened in 2011 by founder and CEO Roger Wade, the mall will be open for the next four years. Constructed of stripped and refitted shipping containers, Boxpark is filled with a mix of fashion and lifestyle brands, galleries, cafés and restaurants. The nearest Tube stations are Old Street and Liverpool Street.

Chapter 8: Where To Stay

Finding the right accommodation can be crucial to any trip. After all, after an exciting day of exploring London, you want to have a suitable place to rest. London has no shortage of choice; best rated hotels or budget accommodation – whichever you prefer. The hotel scene is ever expanding with recent openings including boutique hotels and stylish B&B accommodation in the pretty neighborhoods of Notting Hill and Chelsea as well as more centrally in Bloomsbury and Mayfair.

45 Park Lane located in Mayfair has been transformed into a monument to Art Deco by New York-based designer Thierry Despont. Its exterior is wrapped in striking metal fins. Inside, a double-height ground floor houses the modern American steak restaurant CUT at 45 Park Lane, by chef Wolfgang Puck. They offer park-facing bedrooms and some of the largest hotel rooms in the city, all decorated in warm natural tones and furnished with dark woods, suede and leather.

51 Buckingham Gate, Taj Suites and Residences Gate is a hotel with three restaurants (including the Michelin-starred Quilon Restaurant and Bar) and 24-hour room service. However, all the suites and apartments - which vary in size from one to four bedrooms - have extremely well-equipped kitchens. Other facilities include a spa, butler service and baby-sitting. Buckingham Palace is a five-minute walk away and Westminster Abbey, Trafalgar Square and the Houses of Parliament are not much further. St James's Park is the closest tube station to this hotel.

Ace Hotel at 100 Shoreditch High Street is a big, punchy hotel and a great place to stay for East London, with its buzzy galleries, boutiques and bars, that such has taken root here. Walk into the lobby of the Ace and you'll instantly feel the energy. A reception, coffee shop, bar and lounge rolled into one, it reverberates with the chatter of creatives - from students to CEOs - using it as a work space and meeting place. It's a dark, stripped-back warehouse-style space with barmen in bobble hats and bobos dancing to disco, golden-age hip-hop and electro.

Artist Residence located at 52 Cambridge Street makes a bright new addition to Pimlico, and has a cracking neighborhood restaurant to boot. If you knew everyone else staying here, this 10-room townhouse would be the smartest, easiest house-share ever. There are playful prints from Shoreditch's Pure Evil Gallery on the wall, but it's the food not the art that steals the show. Chef Michael Bremner's 64 Degrees in Brighton has won great acclaim, and the new London outpost does not disappoint.

Chiltern Firehouse located at 1st Chiltern Street in Marylebone is an intimate, 26-room hotel. It's a bit like staying in a cozy private home with brilliant house staff. There's a 24-hour kitchen, and enormous windows overlooking one of London's prettiest streets. There are big bedrooms with gas fireplaces and sexy Sheila Metzner nudes on the walls, and smart marble bathrooms. Sample the best of both London worlds: relaxed and peaceful, but with direct access to the hottest scene in town.

Mondrian London Hotel at 20 Upper Ground is one of 2014's most eagerly anticipated new London hotels. It incorporates hip art gallery Lazarides Editions, and Tate Modern is close by. The rampantly eclectic interiors of the hotel's Dandelyan and rooftop bars and the Curzon-run cinema reference Art Deco, Pop Art and disco. Banquettes are covered in mimosa-yellow velvet; bedrooms boast grey walls and cranberry-pink throws. Metallic finishes ramp up the glamour.

Shangri-La Hotel at the Shard occupies the floors from 34 to 52 of Renzo Piano's 87-floor London landmark. The Shard is sheer alchemy, and a startling treat. This magnificent hotel has some of the best views of London. It's almost a shame the bedrooms (warm, luxuriantly stocked) have any furniture in them at all -

anything that might impede the impact of those views.

The Beaumont Hotel is located at Brown Hart Gardens in Mayfair. The bedrooms are classic and elegant, the studios and suites immaculately clad in high-gloss rosewood and home to more vintage photography and original oil portraits. Alternatively, there's Room, the extraordinary, three-story high sculpture by Antony Gormley which juts out from the front of the hotel and houses just one suite.

The Goring at 15 Beeston Place has been owned and run by the same   family   -

the Gorings - since it opened a little over a century ago. It shows. The hotel possesses a no-expense-spared quirkiness and an idiosyncratic sense of humor for which you will search in vain elsewhere. It is a glorious one-off. The final touch in its recent renovation was unveiled in March 2015 - hand-painted wallpaper by Fromental in the lobby, or the Front Hall, as the Gorings prefer to call it. The 69 rooms and suites are likewise elegant and opulent, from the smallest Splendid Rooms to the silkily sumptuous Belgravia Suites and the duly palatial yet winningly homely Royal Suite, where Kate Middleton is said to have spent her last night as a single woman. The bar is the quintessence of coziness. The private garden is the biggest of its kind in London and as pleasing to contemplate on a rainy day as it is to wander around on a sunny one.

The Ham Yard Hotel is dubbed an Urban Village and constructed around a courtyard which provides not only al fresco dining beside a bronze sculpture of memorable proportion, but specialist shops. Despite the size - 91 bedrooms and suites, 24 apartments, some with private terraces - true to signature style, no two rooms are identical. But the real icing is that - apart from the smiley staff - public spaces are devoid of clues that suggest 'hotel' - this is like a private club, but better.

If you are not into spending that much money on your accommodation, London offers plenty alternatives. Here are some stylish places for under £100.

Photo Credit 85:"Arosfa Hotel" by Stephen McKay Licensed under CC BY-SA 2.0 via Wikimedia Commons

<u>Arosfa Hotel</u> is a 200-year-old Georgian townhouse situated in the historic Bloomsbury district. Now a family-run hotel, it was once the home of the famous artist Sir John Everett Millais. Located in the heart of London, many of the city's main attractions are within walking distance. Oxford Street and The British Museum are 10 minutes away, while Regent's Park can be reached in 25 minutes'

walk. It has become an ideal spot for lovers of words rather than images, with Europe's largest academic bookstore right opposite, a clutch of new and second hand bookshops nearby, and the British Library not too far up the road. The bedrooms have been recently redecorated and there's a garden in which you can read whatever amazing finds you make during the day.

The Church Street Hotel is decorated in a Cuban/Mexican style, with bright colors, arched doorways, wood furniture and hand-painted tiles. This is a fun, exuberant hotel, an unashamedly kitsch yet lovable establishment. The wood-paneled Havana-style lounge offers free organic teas and coffees and a DVD library. The honesty bar has an artisan selection of single malts, rums, spirits and fine wines. The property is 10 minutes' walk from Denmark Hill Overground Station, and a 12-minute bus ride from Oval Tube Station.

The crisp industrial design of this 40-room niche hotel is contemporary and well-priced. Stylotel is a state-of-the-art property set between 2 19th-century townhouses, with ultra-modern, contemporary rooms. Oxford Street is a 15-minute walk away and Hyde Park just a 5-minute walk away. Stylotel is just a 2-minute walk from Paddington Station with its direct rail link services. The Heathrow Express to Heathrow Airport is accessible as well as many other national rail services and access to 4 tube lines.

Twenty Nevern Square is situated in a quiet garden square handily placed for both Earls Court Exhibition Centre and the tube station. Each room is different at this elegant and stylish four-floor brick hotel overlooking a lovely London square. Cozy, but not especially large, rooms are decorated with Asian-style woodwork.

Avo Hotel has turned what was once a newsagent into a very welcoming boutique hotel. Family-run, it has just six rooms, all with mango-wood furnishings and gleaming black-and-grey bathrooms. Islington is 2.2 km from Avo Hotel, while Hoxton Square is 2.2 km from the property. The nearest airport is London City Airport, 10 km from the property. Dalston, which has firmly established itself as the trendy bit of Hackney, now also comes with its own shiny new tube station. But the Avo is also handy for trips to the Hackney Empire, and for getting down with the hipsters at the London Fields lido.

Hotel 55 is a boutique hotel just a 2-minute walk from North Ealing Tube Station. Situated in the Ealing district in London, 4.3 km from Wembley Stadium, Hotel 55 boasts a terrace and a minimalist illuminated garden. There's also a Momo Japanese restaurant downstairs and a 24-hour lounge bar featuring work by Sudhir Deshpande. Its 26 bedrooms, done out in muted colors with all mod cons, make for excellent crash pads. This stylish accommodation with free internet is 30 minutes from central London by underground.

Arran House Hotel is located in the heart of elegant Bloomsbury. This Georgian townhouse is just 5 minutes' walk from The British Museum. Guests can enjoy full English breakfasts, and free Wi-Fi. The 30 rooms range from basic singles with shared facilities to bright, well-furnished doubles with bathrooms. There is a cozy lounge at the front and gorgeous gardens at the back, perfect for a few drinks or a quiet read. Guests can use the microwave, fridge and dining room. Euston Square Underground Station is just a 5-minute walk away, while King's Cross Station is a 15-minute walk. Regent's Park and Oxford Street are both 15 minutes away on foot.

The Hoxton burst on to the scene a few short years ago and has scooped a hatful of awards already. Though its designer chic stylings can still be pretty pricey during the week, on Sundays the rates go into free fall if you book up early. The Hoxton Grill restaurant is run in partnership with the Soho House Group and serves American-style food from breakfast through to dinner with room service options available. There's a bar, big lobby area and outdoor courtyard covered for year round use. Old Street Tube

Station is only 5 minutes' walk away, providing easy access to London's main attractions.

The Pavilion is perfect for those after something a little eccentric. Each room has a different garish theme in a thrift-store style. It's a little dark and makeshift but the price, great location and quirky atmosphere more than make up for it.

Jesmond Hotel is another example of a cracking good value Bloomsbury hotel. The place is elegantly furnished throughout, with many of the bedrooms retaining their original fireplaces complete with marble surrounds. The 15 guest rooms – a dozen with bathroom – are basic but clean and cheerful, and it has a small, pretty garden. There's laundry service and free Wi-Fi.

Chapter 9: London For Foodies

A trip to London wouldn't be complete without experiencing some its finest restaurants and best food markets. The diverse cultural dynamism influenced London's culinary scene in the most creative and imaginative ways, making food markets and restaurants a must when in London.

<u>Chick 'N' Sours</u> is a funky little space in Haggerston, one of London's most exciting neighborhoods for food right now. Ex-DJ and chef Carl Clarke gave the ultimate American soul food an Asian twist. Chick 'N' Sours' highlight is the Bun, a towering inferno of Korean-spiced chicken with chili vinegar, mayo and slaw. Sam Dunne, formerly of Milk & Honey, has conjured up the cocktail list, creating a delicious menu definitely worth trying.

<u>Josè Pizarro</u> is the third restaurant from Spanish chef Josè Pizarro, whose tiny tapas and sherry bar in Bermondsey Street is no longer a neighborhood secret. Pizarro is a much larger site (Josè Tapas Bar is a bit of a squash) in the City, but the sharing-plate menu is along the same lines. If you are wandering around in the City, go to Broadgate Circle. But if you are looking for a more romantic ambiance, check out the place at Bermondsey Street. And while there, don't forget to enjoy the wines; the Spanish wine list is helpfully split into regions, from Rioja to Ribera del Duero, described as the country's quiet star.

<u>Taberno do Mercado</u> has a low-key vibe, filled with wild flowers and low-slung light bulbs in Spitalfields. Nuno Mendes, the chef of the place has gone back to his roots with a restaurant dedicated to Portugal. The highlight of the house are the house-tinned cod cheeks with a chili kick, coming as a fresh take on the nation's love affair with tinned fish. Chefs, including Nuno himself help explain the

wine menu as they deliver dishes around the small restaurant space. The Clip do Monte da Vaia at just £24 is excellent value.

The Ivy at Covent Garden is back after a five-month redesign. Green velvet booths now surround a clever triangular bar in the centre of the room with red leather stools. Now there's a nod to Asia from chef Gary Lee, with new dishes such as miso blackened salmon and yellowfin tuna sashimi. The baked Alaska for two, wheeled out on a silver trolley before being set on fire with flaming rum, then served with more flaming kirsch-soaked cherries, is definitely the highlight of the place. The wine list is reasonable and well arranged; there's a short list for those who can't be bothered to pour through the whole thing. If you're lucky enough to have bagged a table, make the most of it. The attentive waiters won't rush you so opt for a Champagne cocktail as an aperitif.

Le Chabanais in Paris is noted for sparking a restaurant revolution by offering exceptional food at affordable prices. Now chef-owner Inaki Aizpitarte has brought his open-to-all bistro concept to London. Chef Paul Boudier has left Paris to head up the new kitchen in Mayfair. A departure from the popular set menu at the original, Le Chabanais has an à la carte menu, with simple dishes such as

Spanish squid stew, cod with white asparagus and pil pil sauce, and strawberry and rose tart.

London has some of the best street food markets and it would be a shame to skip them. Opening in mid-June 2015 Dinerama at Shoreditch Yard will have six street food 'micro diners' and six food shacks from the likes of B.O.B.'s Lobster (for old-school lobster rolls), BBQ Lab (for hanger-steak burgers) and Breddos tacos (for fried cod-cheek tacos). There will also be six bars, including a rooftop rum shack and a tequila container, and a huge seating area to accommodate the hungry East London hordes.

Model Market at Lewisham High Street is giving NYC's Chelsea a run for its money this summer, with its very own High Line. The so-named rooftop bar and terrace is one of the many new elements to this year's Model Market. There are five drinking spots in the 1950s former market space, including Winyl, a record shop/wine bar, and the tiny blink-and-you-miss-it Rum Shack. Soak up all the booze with juicy burgers from Mother Flipper (the huge Double Candy Bacon Flipper is a winner) and - if you can handle it - finish with a sweet treat from local bakery SE Brownie Bar or real-fruit ice cream from Scoopsy Daisy.

Street Feast has returned to its Dalston HQ for another season. The neon signs and fairy lights have been turned back on, the smell of barbecuing ribs and sizzling burgers is in the air, and the foodie crowds are flocking back. With top-notch stalls such as Mama's Jerk and Yum Bun serving up the favorites (spicy wings, sticky pork-belly buns) and giant cocktails, it's a great night out.

Southbank Centre Market, right beside the concrete corners of the 1950s Royal Festival Hall, serves up a taste of global street food every weekend, from Spanish churros to chickpea-tagine-stuffed wraps. This summer, as part of Alchemy, the Southbank Centre's festival of South-east Asian culture, alfresco-food mavericks KERB will roll out an 11-day event with extra fire and spice. There will be feather-light dosa snacks from Horn OK Please and chili-laced bhangra burgers from Baba G's. Cool down with creamy lassis, gin and tonics and India pale ales, and heat right back up again with a delicious tea dispensed by ever-cheery chai wallahs.

Urban Food Fest is conveniently positioned across the road from the Ace Hotel. This no-frills market is great for a pre- or even post-Shoreditch pub crawl as it's open until midnight and has a weekly changing selection of stalls. The ones to look out for are The Joint - top chef Tom Kerridge is a fan of the towering pulled pork sandwich in a fig-and-vanilla bun, and Holy Toast, which serves a mean mushroom-stuffed grilled cheese sandwich. The perky bar staff serve bottles of Prosecco and Vedett Belgian beers, and musicians strum guitars to create a laid-back vibe.

No matter what the street food trend or en vogue haute cuisine may be, if Londoners are hip to it then it's bound to be found in Soho. Long known as the epicenter of London nightlife, over the years Soho has transformed into the most promising area to eat as well. Here you'll find the densest concentration of excellent cafes, specialty shops, casual eateries, and upscale restaurants in all of London. During the week, Berwick Street Market offers passers excellent options for eating on-the-go. And, of course, Chinatown is just steps away on the other side of Shaftesbury Avenue.

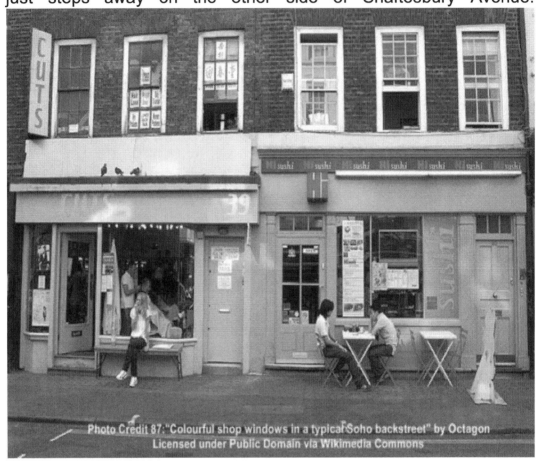

Photo Credit 87: "Colourful shop windows in a typical Soho backstreet" by Octagon
Licensed under Public Domain via Wikimedia Commons

Chapter 10: Nightlife and Clubbing in London

Photo Credit 88:"Chinatown, London" by Aurelien Guichard
Licensed under CC BY-SA 2.0 via Wikimedia Commons

Briefly summarizing London's nightlife is a bit like trying to sum up the city overall: it's practically impossible. The city is too big and varied to say anything briefly with total conviction. All that can safely be said is that London's nightlife really does cater for all tastes and moods. It runs the full gamut from the very wildest drinking dens and clubs to more sedate, laidback spots.

As a general rule, budget travelers - and indeed anyone in search of a proper night out - should avoid the West End. Chinatown may be great for dining, Shaftesbury Avenue has its theaters and Covent Garden is charming, but there are few glimpses of real, authentic London nightlife here. For those backpackers serious about their music, Camden Town is the place to head for live gigs. Stretching away either side of Camden Road, small seedy pubs and bars are interspersed with some seriously good venues, all with a brilliantly bohemian feel.

But as with everything in London, this comes with one notable exception to the rule: Soho. Soho is a titan of the London night; gaudily-lit strip clubs and sex shops vie with achingly cool cocktail bars, smart members' clubs, hip cellar bars and age-old London institutions. Lying to the north of touristy Leicester Square, Soho is also the center of London's gay scene with its main promenade, Old Compton Street, the hub of gay life in the city. To go on a night out in Soho is to really catch the many distinct flavors of the city after dark.

As I already mentioned, summarizing London's nightlife is impossible, but here is a small list of clubs worth checking out.

Located underneath railway arches in Shoreditch, <u>Cargo</u> is at the centre of East London's music scene. This cool venue housed under railway arches showcases an incredibly diverse range of music to a warm and friendly crowd. Cargo's tasty global street food canteen is not to be missed either. The venue also hosts regular DJ nights and offers a tasty bar menu.

Photo Credit 91:"Cargo, Shoreditcht" By Ewan Munro Licensed under CC BY-SA 2.0 via Wikimedia Commons

One of London's first warehouse venues, in the last 10 years, Corsica Studios has become a highly regarded and award-winning venue. It offers a diverse events program, from top promoters to in-house club nights. Expect an arty, friendly crowd including plenty of students. Corsica Studios is located in South London and offers two rooms of music and a bar. A great choice if you're into dubstep and garage. This is the place to go for new, exciting and experimental sounds.

A venue like no other, Egg London continues to push the boundaries. It's a stylish venue spread across three intimate floors. Reminiscent of an Ibiza club, it's the outdoor courtyard that really makes Egg stand out. Cool off, chill out and have a drink under the night sky. With the best music from the world's greatest DJs, mixing with the best sound and lighting available, this club combines a variety of spaces indoors and outdoors along with a 24 hour license. With an eclectic mix of nights, there's something for all kinds of dance music fans to enjoy.

Electric Brixton opened its doors in September 2011 following a million pound investment, maintaining many of the club's original features and installing a new sound system. This is one of South London's best dance venues, hosting regular drum'n'bass, electronica and dance nights, plus big name DJs and live acts.

Fabric is probably the best club in London if not the world, but make sure you like your nights hardcore! If it all gets a bit much, recline on the huge leather chill-out beds and meet some new pals. You can party at Fabric on Friday, Saturday and even Sunday nights. Fabric is playing a variety of electro, house music, breakbeat, and drum'n'bass.

Three floors, a great sound system and crazy light shows in the main room - <u>Heaven</u> is a club for people that really want to party. Heaven is one of London's largest and most famous gay clubs. So, dance the night away with the drag queens at Heaven, London's great big electro-pop, house and dance nightclub. Formerly the legendary Camden Palace, <u>KOKO</u> is a 1,500 capacity club, hosting both live music and club events. The building has undergone a massive refurbishment program and been restored to its original theatrical style, with six bars, a stage and a dance floor. KOKO's rooftop bar is open during summer. Camden's multi-layered KOKO nightclub boasts a full events calendar of live music and DJ-led club nights, including the popular Buttoned Down Disco, Guilty Pleasures, and Club NME. Playing to a range of musical tastes, KOKO's music policy covers everything from rock and pop to blues and dance music.

Photo Credit 93:""The Koko Club" by Oxyman Licensed under Public Domain via Wikimedia Commons

Ministry Of Sound is one of London's most popular nightclubs. They host nights featuring house, techno and occasionally indie rock and drum and bass. This club has been entertaining club-goers for 20 years, spawning a record label in the process. Ministry of Sound boasts four bars, four dance floors and five distinctive rooms and still draws big names such as Paul Oakenfold, Judge Jules and Tall Pall.

Book tickets in advance and get there early to avoid the long queues.

Enjoy summer parties at <u>Studio 338</u>. This venue in North Greenwich, a short walk from The O2, is London's biggest club and includes an open, heated terrace, where a host of top acts perform. On colder nights you can either party on the heated terrace or move inside.

<u>XOYO</u> is a unique events space in the Shoreditch area of east London where you can enjoy live acts, art exhibitions and some of the best musical experiences in the capital. Many cutting edge DJs and dance music acts have played at the venue. This two-room

nightclub, art space and upstairs cafe bar close to the Old Street roundabout in Shoreditch is renowned for being cutting edge.

Conclusion

London served as a great inspiration for all kinds of artists during the centuries. Many writers were inspired and wrote about London, yet somehow, to really get the feeling all of them are talking about, London should be visited. No book can picture the beautiful diversity of this city.

Whether you travel on a small budget or a big one, London offers so much for every taste and desire. Although I did my best to present London's highlights in this short travel guide, somehow, looking over the written pages, I feel like I didn't even scratch the surface of all the things London offers. But I hope this guide will point you in the right direction on your London adventure.

PS: Please leave your review

If you reached this last page, probably this travel guide has given you some ideas about your stay in London!!

Would you be kind enough to leave a review for this book on Amazon? It will help other travelers to find their way through this beautiful country!

Many thanks and enjoy your trip!

Thanks a lot.

Made in United States
Troutdale, OR
03/16/2025

29787979R00113